1 MONTH OF
FREE
READING

at

www.ForgottenBooks.com

By purchasing this book you are eligible for one month membership to ForgottenBooks.com, giving you unlimited access to our entire collection of over 1,000,000 titles via our web site and mobile apps.

To claim your free month visit:

www.forgottenbooks.com/free190618

ISBN 978-0-265-19263-4
PIBN 10190618

The Cambridge Manuals of Science and
Literature

THE HISTORY OF THE ENGLISH BIBLE

CAMBRIDGE UNIVERSITY PRESS

London: FETTER LANE, E.C.

C. F. CLAY, Manager

Edinburgh: 100, PRINCES STREET

Berlin: A. ASHER AND CO.

Leipzig: F. A. BROCKHAUS

New York: G. P. PUTNAM'S SONS

Bombay and Calcutta: MACMILLAN AND CO., Ltd.

THE
HISTORY
OF THE
ENGLISH BIBLE

BY

JOHN BROWN, D.D.

Cambridge :
at the University Press
1911

Cambridge:

PRINTED BY JOHN CLAY, M.A.

AT THE UNIVERSITY PRESS.

With the exception of the coat of arms at the foot, the design on the title page is a reproduction of one used by the earliest known Cambridge printer John Siberch 1521

PREFACE

THE celebration of the Tercentenary of the Authorised Version of the English Bible of 1611 has called into existence the little book here presented to the reader's notice. It is the brief repetition of a story beginning in 670 A.D. and reaching on for twelve hundred years to 1870. It takes us back to the Monastery of Whitby where Cædmon the monk paraphrased Scripture story in Saxon song, and brings us through the centuries to the Abbey of Westminster where a distinguished body of English scholars met in 1870 and commenced that Revision of the Scriptures which first saw the light in 1881. The History of the English Bible, like the Records of Bunyan's House Beautiful, is "the history of many famous things, as of things both Ancient and Modern." It is a tale of devoted service rendered often by men in loneliness and exile; of faithfulness even to martyrdom and death on the part of those who counted not their lives dear unto them, if only they could serve the great cause of spiritual enlightenment; it tells of great gifts of

mind and great attainments in scholarship couse-
crated to the sacred cause of truth and the elevation
of mankind. It will be found that our Greatest Book
has a great history of its own, apart from the nature
of its contents. It is not too much to say that to the
men who have rendered such high service to the
English-speaking people here at home and in our
wide-spread Empire abroad, we owe it that their
memory shall not perish, or their names be forgotten.

J. B.

HAMPSTEAD
11 *March* 1911

CONTENTS

LIST OF PLATES

CHAPTER I

LOOKED at from the human side the Christian religion was established at first, and made permanent in history afterwards, by means of two institutions—the Church and the Bible. The Church came before the Bible, for the simple reason that life must exist before there can be any description of it, but the Bible was indispensable to the true development of the Church. The witness borne by the Apostles to the Life, Death and Resurrection of their Lord was the appointed human means of creating the Church: "the Life was manifested," said they, "and we have seen and bear witness and declare unto you the Life, the Eternal Life." So far as men received this witness and believed, the Church of God became a great fact and took its place in history. Then came the question of its perpetuation and permanent direction. Even Apostles could not always live and bear their testimony, and if that testimony were committed solely to the keeping of mere tradition it would be changed

B.   1

and weakened as it passed from lip to lip. Thus arose the need for the Bible as well as the Church. By way of repeating and perpetuating the witness of the Apostles the Church spreads the Bible, and in return the Bible builds up the Church, preventing false developments, guarding against erroneous bye-paths, and bringing Christian life and practice ever and again to the test of a divine standard. In short, the Bible is for the men of all the centuries what the personal witness of the Apostles was to the men of the first—the proclamation of the great creative acts of God for man's salvation.

And to be effective it must be, as at Pentecost, a proclamation to every man in his own language wherein he was born. Both the personal testimony and the written word, both the missionary and the Bible must speak to men in their own tongue. This was felt from the first in the Christianisation of our own land. When in the spring of 597 A.D. Augustine and his forty companions came from Rome as missionaries and landed on the coast of Kent, it was through their Frankish interpreters they made known to King and people the purpose of their coming. And as they needed an interpreter so did the Bible they brought with them, for that Bible was the Latin Vulgate of Jerome, to all intents and purposes a sealed book to our Saxon forefathers. Thus arose the need and also the fact of an English Bible, the rise and development of which it is the purpose of these pages to narrate.

The political constitution under which we live, it has often been said, was not made but grew, that it is what it is as the outcome of a process of development, the result of many a struggle with adverse forces, and so has become in itself the record as it is the result of the historic past. Now that which is true of the English constitution is true also of the English Bible. It has arrived at its present form through many successive stages of growth, and each of these stages presents its own features of historic interest, and its own record of self-sacrificing zeal and devotion.

As we might expect it is not easy to speak both with certainty and fulness as to the beginnings of our English Bible in Anglo-Saxon times. For they belong to a dim and distant past and there are but scanty records to light us on our way. More than that they had their rise in days of invasion and wild confusion, days when the Danes, in successive raids which recur with melancholy monotony through a whole generation, ravaged the land from east to west and from north to south. They not only desolated the Midland shires and stormed and looted the cities of the West, but also plundered the monasteries of Northumbria, those homes of learning, the manuscripts they found there being of small account in the eyes of these rovers from across the sea. There was also another agency at work almost equally disastrous to the cause of sacred learning. Within less than seventy years of the landing of Augustine, as Bede tells us, the terrible plague of 664 A.D. raged with especial severity in the monasteries both of men and women. At Lindisfarne, at Ely, at Wearmouth and Jarrow, at Carlisle, at Barking, and at Lastingham in the East Riding of York, this pestilence carried off nearly all the inmates. The effect of this on Scripture learning could not but be most disastrous.

Yet, after all, it is to this very period that scholars have assigned the first rude beginnings of what may perhaps be called a Saxon version of the Scriptures, simple metrical paraphrases, rather than ordered translation. These were the work of Cædmon, the monk of Whitby, whose date lies between 658 and 680 A.D., and whose active period may be assigned to about 670 A.D. He has been called the first Saxon poet, though he cannot now be credited with all that was once claimed for him. A clue discovered by a German professor in 1857, being followed up, led to other discoveries, with the result that now, by the general consent of scholars, many poems formerly attributed to Cædmon are reclaimed for his fellow-Northumbrian, Cynewulf, who belonged to the century after him. Still it was Cædmon who began to set forth Scripture paraphrases in the Saxon tongue. All we know of his personal history we get from a single chapter of Bede's *Ecclesiastical History* (iv. 24), where he is described as an unlearned man of great piety and humility who had received by divine grace such a gift of sacred poetry that he was able after short meditation to render into English verse whatever passage was translated to him out of the Latin Scriptures. This unlettered peasant, being taken as a monk into the monastery at Whitby, under the rule of the Abbess Hilda, was there instructed in the history of the Old and New Testaments, with the result that what was translated to him out of the Vulgate he reproduced from time to time in beautiful and touching verse: "so that his teachers were glad to become his hearers." We are told that he sang of the creation of the world and the origin of mankind, of the departure of Israel from Egypt and their entrance into Canaan, and also of many other parts of the older Scriptures. It is said that he also para-. phrased portions of the New Testament, singing of the Lord's incarnation, passion, resurrection and as-cension ; of the coming of the Holy Spirit, and the teaching of the Apostles of our Lord. So far as these metrical versions of the Scriptures are known to us we owe that knowledge to a tenth century manuscript in the Bodleian, bequeathed to that library by the Earl of Arundel. The first part of this manuscript is in one handwriting, and contains paraphrases of portions of the books of Genesis, Exodus and Daniel; the second part consists of three poems, the first relating to the Fall of the Angels and the Temptation of Man—a daring and original product of his genius which has led to his being described as "the Milton of our forefathers." These paraphrases being in the native tongue of the people were learnt and sung by them and thus became their sole source of Bible knowledge. Bede, who told us about Cædmon, relates also that he' himself translated the Creed and the Lord's Prayer into the Saxon tongue; and we cannot forget the pathetic story of his dictating to a scribe, in the last hours of his life, a translation of the closing chapter of the Gospel of John.

From Anglo-Saxon times there have come down to us versions of the Psalter, the Four Gospels and the Pentateuch. The Psalter is thought to have been translated about the end of the seventh century or the beginning of the eighth, and to be the work of Aldhelm, Bishop of Sherborne some time before 709 A.D. This version survives in a single MS. preserved in the National Library in Paris, Psalms i.–li. being rendered in prose, the remainder in verse. There have been three reprints in modern times of this complete Psalter.

Next to this comes the important question of the Four Gospels existing in Anglo-Saxon, Northumbrian

Incipit euangeliu scdm Iohannem·

IN PRINCIPIO ERAT UERBU· ET UERBU ERAT APUD DM·
& ds erat uerbu· Hocerat inprincipio· apud dm· ert·

Nfruman pæs popo ⁊þ popo pæs mid gode· ⁊god pæs
þ popo· ⁊þ pæs onfruman ↄ mid gode· ealle þing
pæron ge porhtæ þurhhyne ⁊nan þing næs ge porht
butan hym· þ pæs lyf þeon hym ge porht pæs ⁊þ lyf
pæs manna leoht· ⁊þ leoht lyht on þystru· ⁊þ ystro
ne genamon· man pæs fra gode asend· þæs nama
pæs iohannes· þes com to ge pitnysse· þ hit ge pitnysse
cydor· be þa leohte þ ealle men þurhhyne ge lyfdon·

man on þysne middan eard· he pæs on middan
eard· ⁊middan eard pæs ge porht þurh hyne·
⁊middan eard hyne ne ge cneop· To hys agnu
he co· ⁊hig hyne ne unoffi fengon· Sodlice spa
hpylce spa hyne unoffi fengon· he sealde hym
anpeald· þ hig pæron godes bearn þa ðe ge lyfað
on hys naman þa ne synd acennede of bloodum
ne of flæsce pyllan· ne of þ hiffi· achig synd of gode
acennede· And þ popo pæs flæsc ge hopofi· ⁊purode
on us· ⁊pe ge sapon hys puldor· spylce an cennedf·
pillan

and Old Mercian versions. Professor Skeat is of opinion that there was but one Anglo-Saxon version and that five out of the six MSS. of the Gospels now left to us, though written in different places, are intimately connected with each other, and derived from that original, now lost. The six referred to are (1) the *Corpus* MS. preserved in the library of Corpus Christi College, Cambridge; (2) the *Cambridge* MS. presented to the University Library by Archbishop Parker in 1574; (3) the *Bodley* MS. in the Bodleian Library; of this there is an exact duplicate in the British Museum, both agreeing closely with the Corpus MS.; (4) the *Cotton* MS. written early in the 11th century. This suffered serious injury in the fire which in 1731 partially destroyed the Cotton Library, then deposited at Ashburnham House, Westminster. (5) The *Hatton* MS. in the Bodleian, which gives the Gospels in the following order—Mark, Luke, Matthew, John; (6) the *Royal* MS. now in the Royal Library in the British Museum. The handwriting of this copy is bold, hasty and rough, while that of the Hatton MS., which seems to have been copied from it, is in an exceedingly uniform, upright and clear hand. The Cotton MS. again, exhibits the text in its earliest, and the Hatton MS. in its latest form.

Besides these six Anglo-Saxon versions of the Four Gospels, two Anglo-Saxon *Glosses* to the Latin text have come down to us—the *Lindisfarne Gospels*

and the *Rushworth Gospels.* It may be explained
that a gloss differs from a translation in that it con-
strues the text word for word, between the lines,
without much regard to the grammatical arrangement. It simply supplies a clue to the meaning of
the words of the original separately. The *Lindisfarne
Gospels,* also known as the Durham Book, is one of
the most valued treasures in our national collection,
being one of the Cotton MSS. in the British Museum.
It consists of 258 leaves of thick vellum, and contains the Four Gospels in Latin with an interlinear
Northumbrian gloss. The Latin text was written in
the island of Lindisfarne by Eadfrith the bishop,
about 700 A.D. in honour of his predecessor St
Cuthbert, and so is sometimes known as St Cuthbert's Gospels. The interlinear gloss in the Northumberland dialect is probably more than two centuries
later, and was the work of a monk named Aldred.
This MS. is elaborately ornamented with paintings of
the Evangelists; and with full-page cruciform designs,
borders and initial letters, in the style introduced
from Ireland. It was kept at Lindisfarne, the Holy
Isle of Northumberland, until the Danish invasion of
Northumbria, when it was carried away for safety.
It afterwards remained for a long time at Durham,
and then was restored to the Priory of Lindisfarne,
where it was preserved until the Dissolution of the
Monasteries. Purchased by Sir Robert Cotton in the

17th century, it passed through him to the keeping of the British Museum.

The *Rushworth Gospels* was so named because presented to the Bodleian Library by John Rushworth of-Lincoln's Inn, who was deputy clerk to the House of Commons during the Long Parliament. It was originally copied from the Vulgate by Mac Regol, an Irish priest, about 820 A.D. The interlinear gloss was added about a century later by two men, a scribe named Owun and Farman a priest of Harewood on the river Wharfe. It may be mentioned that the gloss in this MS., but throughout the first Gospel only, is in the Old Mercian dialect, and therefore of peculiar interest as giving us an example of a dialect, of which the specimens are extremely scarce, and yet which is closely related to the modern literary language.

It may be well at this point to emphasise the fact that the time when the Psalter and the Four Gospels were given to the people in their own Saxon tongue was the 7th century—the century described as the time of greatest advance previous to the Norman Conquest. Between the coming of Augustine in 597 A.D. and the conversion of the people of Sussex under Wilfrid in 686 A.D. lies the long spiritual campaign for the conversion of the entire people from heathenism to Christianity. It was the century of Paulinus, of the great and good missionary bishop

Aidan, who founded the monastery of Lindisfarne ; and of Cuthbert who fills so large a space in the memories of the people of England, especially of northern England, the region where Christianity won some of its greatest victories. It was the century, too, in which the great churchman, Theodore of Tarsus, came to this island where, as we are told, he made his copious stores of learning, both sacred and secular, available for the people. We read of the multitude of disciples who flocked to his daily lectures and of the knowledge, along with that of the sacred Scriptures, which he imparted to his hearers. "Nor in fact," we are told, "were there ever happier times since the days when the English first landed in Britain...the desires of men were strongly directed towards the new-found joys of the heavenly kingdom ; and all who desired to be instructed in the sacred Scriptures had teachers near at hand who could impart to them that knowledge."

Unfortunately the flood tide of that century was followed by the ebb tide of the next. There is no mistaking the fact that in the period between the death of the Venerable Bede in 735 A.D. and the birth of King Alfred in 848 A.D. the intellect and heart of England had suffered a sad relapse into ignorance and barbarism. There was a general decline of civilisation and learning, the light becoming obscured by the superstitions and impious fabrications which began to prevail.

Various causes may be assigned for so disastrous a decline. Under the ravages of the great plague many of the East Saxons relapsed for a time into idolatry; again, later there was a further outbreak from which Bede's own monastery of Jarrow suffered severely, the pestilence carrying off all the monks who could read or preach or sing the antiphons. It was also a time of discord and revolution in the government. In the course of that century fifteen kings of Northumbria swayed the sceptre, and of these, five were deposed, five murdered, and two voluntarily abdicated the throne. Then too there were the persistent inroads of the Danes followed by the destruction of the monasteries and of the MSS. they contained. A monk of Peterborough pathetically relates that when Inguar and Ubba came to his abbey "they burned and brake, slew abbot and monks, and so dealt with what they found there, which was erewhile full rich, that they brought it to nothing." But worst of all there followed a general debasement of morals. One serious sign of this was the founding by wealthy laymen of pseudo-monasteries, unholy convents, in which freed from the restraints of law they lived their lives of licentious ease, and under the pretence of a religious life, evaded the duties of the public service. Such was the state of things when King Alfred came to the throne in 871.ˈ It is not surprising that in such a time of reaction the work of Bible translation made no advance beyond the version of the Psalter and of the Lindisfarne Gospels of the century before. We have now to notice that the next step forward was taken by King Alfred himself. To his enlightened mind it was an unspeakable sorrow that the nation had so seriously sunk backward. He says: "Formerly men came from beyond our borders, seeking wisdom in our own land; now, if we are to have it at all, we must look for it abroad. So great was the decay of learning among Englishmen that there were very few on this side Humber, and I ween not many north of it, who could understand the ritual, or translate a letter from Latin into English. No, I cannot remember one such, south of the Thames, when I came to the throne."

King Alfred did not, as some men do, content himself with mourning the degeneracy of the days. He resolutely set out to bring about a better time. He aimèd at the creation of a native literature and for this purpose sought the aid of learned ecclesiastics beyond his own borders. From Wales he invited Asser, his future biographer; from Mercia he imported Plegmund and Werferth; from Omer came Grimbald, and from the lands near the mouth

of the Elbe came John the Old Saxon, whose an-
cestors were heathen, but who was himself a learned
ecclesiastic.   With the aid of these men he enriched
his people with translations of some of the great
works which Rome had given to the world.   He
himself translated Gregory's *Regula Pastoralis*,
setting forth the character, duties and special tempta-
tions of the Christian pastor.   He describes the mode
of translation—"sometimes word for word, and sometimes meaning for meaning, as I learned the sense."
Bede's *Ecclesiastical History* also was translated
from Latin into Saxon, either by Alfred's own hand
or under his supervision.   But what we are most
concerned with now is the fact that he translated for
his people certain chapters from the Old Testament and a passage from the New.   In publishing
his Laws, called "Alfred's Dooms," he appended to
them almost the whole of four chapters of the book of
Exodus (xx.—xxiii.) containing the Ten Commandments and the Mosaic code of civil law in all its
archaic simplicity.   Following this came a reference
to the mission of "the Lord's Son, our God, who is
Jesus Christ, who came into the world, not to destroy
the law but to fulfil it, and to increase it with all
good things."   Then came a description of the Council
of Jerusalem as given in the fifteenth chapter of the
Acts of the Apostles and a rehearsal of its decrees.
The acts of this Council end with the Golden Rule as
inserted in *Codex Bezae*—"And that which ye will

that other men should not do to you, do ye not to other men." He then proceeds to set before his people what he considers the source of all legislation, the divine ordinances given amidst the thunders of Sinai, and shows how that law was modified by the teaching of Christ.

Before leaving the Anglo-Saxon period of our history mention must be made of one other work which belongs to it, a metrical version of the Penta-teuch and the Book of Joshua, partly translated and partly epitomised by Ælfric Abbot of Peterborough in 1004, and Archbishop of York in 1023. It is some-times known as "Ælfric's Heptateuch" and it has been suggested that it is probably part only of a much larger work, inasmuch as there are translations of the Books of Kings, Esther, Job, Judith, the Maccabees and of the Four Gospels in existence which appear to be of the same date, and are supposed to be from the same pen. A copy of Ælfric's version in the British Museum is illustrated with numerous drawings in body-colour and outline lightly tinted. It is in vellum, in folio, and is an early 11th century MS. The story of Joseph is given with illustrations depicting his entertainment of his brethren in Egypt, and the putting of the cup into Benjamin's sack. So far did Bible ver-sions and Bible reading go in Anglo-Saxon days before the Norman conquerors reached our shores.

CHAPTER II

WITH the Conquest of England by the Normans there arose, of necessity, urgent problems for the conquered land to deal with. Not the least was the question as to what should be the language of the future: Should it be that of the conquered or the conqueror? Before the powerful forces wielded by King and Court, and by the incoming social elements of Norman society, the English language had to fight for its very existence. But it fought strenuously and its sturdy character stood it in good stead. And so it came to pass that while Norman-French became the language of the Court, the School and the Bar, the Saxon tongue held its place tenaciously in farm-house and cottage, in the transactions of the market-place and in the every-day proceedings of common life.

But while this is true it will be seen that but little could be done in the way of translating into English the Scriptures of the Latin Vulgate. The

Anglo-Saxon version of the Four Gospels continued to be written as late as the 12th century. In the British Museum there is a copy which was evidently written towards the end of that century. There are other copies also in existence at Oxford, Cambridge and elsewhere, showing that the more ancient form of the English language continued to be in use long after the Conquest. Still, up to the year 1360 only one book of Scripture had been entirely rendered into English since the Conquest. This was the Psalter, which about the year 1320 appeared in two forms. The first was a translation by William de Schorham, vicar of Chart Sutton in the county of Kent. It was followed nearly about the same time by a translation of the Book of Psalms into the Saxon dialect of North Yorkshire, which was accompanied by an English commentary, the work of Richard Rolle, a chantry priest and hermit, of Hampole, near Doncaster. This man, a native of Thornton, near Pickering, was one of the mystics of his time, a deeply spiritual soul of whom we read that he turned great numbers to God by his exhortations, and comforted many by his advice and writings and by the special efficacy of his prayers. This Psalter of his, with its commentary, appears to have been written for the benefit of Margaret Kirkby, a devout recluse at Anderby, and came to be held in high esteem by others, being widely diffused in the century after it was written.

His works exhibit the more spiritual side of one of those movements which led up to the Reformation.

Beyond the versions of portions of Scripture already mentioned nothing was done in the way of giving a complete Bible to the English people until Wycliffe's time.   Indeed we may say that nothing could be done until the language itself had taken something more nearly approaching a permanent form.   Up to the time of the Conquest, and since the days of King Alfred and the learned men he had gathered to his Court, the West Saxon dialect had been gradually winning for itself more and more of literary form.   But with the Conquest that came to an end.   The contest for supremacy between French and English led to wide separations, and there were almost as many English dialects as there were counties.   The centrifugal force always going on in language brought it about that in process of time the northern counties could not understand the southern, or the southern the northern.   Before there could be a common English Bible there must be something approaching to a common English speech.   A unifying centre must somehow be found, and from the nature of the case could only be found in central England, which was in touch both with north and south, and to a considerable extent could understand both. Circumstances from which there could be no appeal rendered it imperative, therefore, that the Bible for

B.   2

all must be a Bible in the Middle England speech, the speech slowly taking definite literary form as the English of Chaucer and Wycliffe. In this way it came about that John Wycliffe was the man, and Lutterworth near Leicester was the place, and the second half of the fourteenth century was the time, to give to the English people the first complete Bible in the English tongue.

Born in the little village of Wycliffe-on-Tees, near Richmond in Yorkshire, Wycliffe went as a student to Oxford where, by learning and ability, he obtained a Fellowship at Merton, the Mastership of Balliol and in 1365 the Wardenship of Archbishop Islip's new foundation in Canterbury Hall. The first half of the fourteenth century was a time of seething opinion in the Church. It was the time of the removal of the Papacy to Avignon and when it advanced claims and exercised powers which plunged Italy and Germany into discord. In opposition to these, John Marsiglio of Padua, in his *Defensor Pacis*, proclaimed ideas which, as time has shown, were to regulate the future progress of Europe. He gave expression to conceptions of the sovereignty of the people and of the official position of the ruler which mark the development of European politics down to our own day. Indeed he defined the limits of ecclesiastical authority and asserted the dignity of the individual believer in advance of what has yet been realised. Whether

Wycliffe came under this man's influence, or worked his way independently to similar conclusions, we may not decisively determine, but in the letter of Pope Gregory XI to Archbishop Sudbury and the Bishop of London, of May 1377, directing proceedings against Wycliffe, he writes as follows: "We have heard forsooth with much grief by the intimation of many credible persons that John Wycliffe, rector of the church of Lutterworth in the diocese of Lincoln, professor of the sacred page...does not fear to assert, profess and publicly proclaim certain propositions and conclusions which (albeit with certain change of terms) appear to breathe the perverse opinions and the unlearned doctrine of Marsilius of Padua and John of Jandun, of condemned memory." Before the arrival of this Bull ordering Wycliffe's trial Edward III died; the prelates could not take action thereon before the end of 1377, and when Wycliffe was summoued before the Archbishop and Courtney, Bishop of London, the Council did not think it wise that the trial should proceed.

This Papal prosecution, however, and still more the Great Schism in the Papacy of 1378, produced a very powerful effect upon the mind of Wycliffe. The sight of two Popes each claiming to be Head of the Church, and each devoting his entire energies to the destruction of his rival, shocked his soul, and dealt a heavy blow at that idea of the Unity of the Church

which had exercised so powerful an influence on the
imagination of the Middle Ages. We should be quite
within the truth if we said that the Great Schism of
1378 in the Roman Church had a direct and powerful
effect in the production of the complete English Bible
of 1382. For while it led Wycliffe, more energetically
than before, to denounce a corrupt hierarchy, and the
enslavement of the Church by an antichristian Pope,
it also led him and his followers to set about translating the Bible into English that all men might be
supplied with the means of judging on these questions
for themselves. He held that before all things God's
Word must be taught in its own simplicity. He
taught that Christ and His Apostles converted the
world by making known the truths of Scripture in a
form familiar to them. There ought, he said, to be a full
and literal translation of the sacred text, for that the
friars were guilty of "docking and clipping the Word
of God, and tattering it by their rime." To move the
English there must be an English Bible. That which
is every man's guide ought to be in every man's hand.
It is a book for all. Besides setting forth the great
seminal truths of theology it takes up the relations,
duties and trials of social and public life. It is a
wise word for the parent and another for the child ;
it gives directions, too, to master and servant. It
breathes promises of special tenderness to what must
always be a very large class—the people in trouble,

the widow, the fatherless, the suffering, the bereaved. It exhorts to those Christian graces without which life would go on heavily—patience and humility, condescension and self-denial, disinterested love and unwearied beneficence. The Bible is thus a people's book, overshadowing with its authority individuals, households, churches and kingdoms; including in its jurisdiction persons of every rank, age and calling, from birth to death, telling all men what to believe, what to obey, and how to suffer. Since then the Bible was for all, Wycliffe resolved that, as far as in him lay, all should have it.

We do not know at what precise time he began the work of translation, but we know that by 1380 he was busy upon the New Testament while his friend Nicholas of Hereford was engaged upon the Old. He probably knew nothing of Greek and therefore his translation was of necessity from the Latin Vulgate. Hereford's work breaks off abruptly in the middle of a verse (Baruch iii. 20), it has been conjectured because of his arrest and trial at Canterbury where he was excommunicated. It should be mentioned here that in the Vulgate Baruch follows the book of Jeremiah and is not relegated to the Apocrypha. The original manuscript of Hereford's translation with his alterations and corrections is preserved in the Bodleian Library. The remaining books of the Old Testament, Ezekiel, Daniel, the twelve Minor Prophets and the two books of the Maccabees were translated by another hand, probably by Wycliffe himself after he had finished the New Testament. The work was completed by the end of the year 1382, two years before the death of Wycliffe, which took place in 1384. It was circulated in various forms and, to render the work more practically useful, tables of the Lessons and of the Epistles and Gospels for Sundays were added to many of the copies. Also some portions of the Bible were transcribed and issued in separate form.

The first Wycliffite version was no sooner completed than its many imperfections became manifest. The desire to be faithful in the rendering of the exact words led the translators into Latinisms having their source in the Vulgate version, so that some parts can scarcely be called English at all. There seems to have been little or no consideration of the idiomatic differences between the Latin and the English tongues. Wycliffe's own part was less defective in this respect than that of Hereford his co-worker, who was more painfully literal in his rendering than his master. The result was that no sooner was the work completed than it was felt it must be done over again, and the work of revision was begun under Wycliffe's own guidance but was not completed till 1388, or four years after his death. Of Wycliffe's Bible, therefore, there are thus an earlier and a later version. This later revision, while directed at the outset by Wycliffe himself, was really the work of a friend and disciple, John Purvey. This man was a native of Lathbury, a village near Newport Pagnell, who during the closing years of Wycliffe's life came to live with him at Lutterworth. This revision of the earlier version, while instigated by Wycliffe, came to be Purvey's great life-work, and in his "General Prologue" he tells us how he set about it. First, he says he had much travail, with divers fellows and helpers, to gather many old Bibles and other doctors and common glosses and to make one Latin Bible "somedeal" true. In other words he sought to get the best form of the Latin text, to begin with. Then next, to study that text anew, the text with the gloss and such other doctors as he might get, and especially Lyra on the Old Testament, that helped him full much in his work. The third thing was to take counsel with old grammarians and old divines concerning hard words and hard sentences, how they might best be understood and translated. The fourth step was to translate as he could according to the meaning and to have many good fellows and cunning at the correcting of the translation. These are his memorable concluding words : "By this manner with good living and great travail men can come to true and clear translating, and true understanding of Holy Writ, seem it never so hard at the beginning. God grant to us all grace to know well and keep well Holy Writ, and suffer joyfully some pain for it at the last ! Amen."

Of course it need hardly be said that before the invention of printing both the earlier and the later versions were accessible only in manuscript; and neither of them appeared *in print* in complete form till 1850. The New Testament in the later version was published by Lewis in 1731, by Baber in 1810, and by Bagster in his English Hexapla in 1841. Of the early version the Song of Solomon was given in a commentary of 1823; and the New Testament of the same version was published by Pickering in 1848. Then in 1850 the Oxford University Press published a complete edition of both versions in parallel columns under the title : "The Holy Bible, containing the Old and New Testaments with the Apocryphal Books in the earliest English versions made from the Latin Vulgate by John Wycliffe and his followers; Edited by the Rev. J. Forshall and Sir F. Madden." This is truly a noble work in four volumes, royal quarto, and beautifully printed. It is the fruit of twenty-two years of labour, as many as 170 MSS. being examined by the editors, and the various readings of some 60 MSS. being given throughout. Obsolete or obscure words are explained in a glossary appended to the fourth volume.

From the time of Purvey's Revision in 1388 to the time of the first printed New Testament by William Tyndale in 1525, or for a period of 137 years, this translation of the Scriptures, known as Wycliffe's

version, though really a joint work by him and his
followers, continued to be copied by professional
scribes, or by private persons for their own use,
either wholly or in portions. Many of these have
come down to us from the 14th and 15th centuries.
Forshall and Madden counted no fewer than 165
copies, 42 of them giving the earlier version ; and
since this enumeration was made in 1850 several more
have come to light. It was a costly work to produce
in its entirety, having to be copied by hand ; but its
multiplication must have been continuous and fairly
rapid. The copies, the numbers of which have just
been given, must have been made within forty or
fifty years of the completion of the revision ; others
have at various times been discovered, but how many
have perished during the process of the centuries it
is impossible to say. Of those that remain nearly
half are of small size, such as could be made the daily
companions of their owners. They were found in the
high places of the land as well as among the common
people. A folio copy of two volumes on vellum, in
the earlier version, which is preserved in the British
Museum, shows painted in the upper part of the illuminated border of the first page the armorial shield
of Thomas of Woodstock, Duke of Gloucester, the
youngest son of Edward III. There is also a copy of
the later version, with illuminated initials and borders,
which belonged to the library of Henry VII, the

initial letter being a red rose, and the ornamental border containing the royal arms and a portcullis. Another copy was presented to Queen Elizabeth as a birthday gift by her chaplain.

It was, however, among the commons of England that the new translation of the Bible in whole or in portions found readiest and most responsive welcome. Leicester is but a walk of a few miles from Lutterworth, and the work of Bible translation in the one town soon made itself felt in the other. Leicester became conspicuous for its sympathy with the opinions and writings of Wycliffe, so much so that Archbishop Courtney came down in 1389 and on the 2nd of November celebrated high mass at the high altar of the monastery in full pontificals. In the course of this celebration, "in solemn wise, by ringing the bells, lighting the candles and putting out the same again, and throwing them down to the ground," he denounced those who favoured the views of Wycliffe. The next day, being All-Souls-day, he made inquiry from ecclesiastics and laymen, when the names of eight persons were laid before him, all of whom he denounced by name as excommunicate and accursed, and ordered this excommunication to be proclaimed in divers parish churches in Leicester. The whole town also was placed under interdict so long as the guilty persons were among its inhabitants, and on the 7th of November the Sheriff was ordered to arrest them under the King's Writ.   Three out of the eight recanted their opinions and were absolved, but before absolution there was to be hard penance.   This penance was that on the next Sunday they were to go before the Cross three times during the procession at the Cathedral Church of our Lady of Leicester. They were to do this "in their shirts, having no other apparel upon them," holding a crucifix in one hand and a taper of wax half a pound weight in the other. The procession being ended they were to stand before the Cross during the whole time of mass with their tapers and crosses in their hands.   As if this were not humiliation enough they were further ordered to stand the following Saturday in the full and public market in the town of Leicester, standing in like manner in their shirts, without any more clothes upon their bodies, holding the aforesaid crosses in their right hands.   Having submitted to all this in the cold November days of 1389 Roger Dexter and William Smith and Alice his wife were finally absolved as stated in letters dated November 17 in the year of our Lord God 1389.   Such were the proceedings which within a twelvemonth signalised the completion and final revision of the Wycliffe Bible.

Passing now over some nineteen years we come to measures more directly assailing the version of the Scriptures with which we are now concerned.   Archbishop Courtney having been succeeded by Archbishop

Arundel, the latter caused certain Constitutions to be enacted in a Convocation of the province of Canterbury held at Oxford in 1408. These Constitutions of Arundel consisted of thirteen Articles, the sixth of which reads as follows : "We will and command that no book or treatise made by John Wycliffe...be from henceforth read in schools, halls, hospitals or other places whatsoever, within our province of Canterbury." This article was supplemented by a seventh which was directly aimed at Wycliffe's Bible. It reads thus : "Item, It is a dangerous thing as witnesseth blessed St Jerome, to translate the text of the Holy Scripture out of the tongue into another ; for in the translation the same sense is not always easily kept, as the same St Jerome confesseth, that although he were inspired, yet oftentimes in this he erred : we therefore decree and ordain that no man, hereafter, by his own authority translate any text of the Scripture into English or any other tongue, by way of a book, libel or treatise; and that no man read any such book, libel or treatise, now lately set forth in the time of John Wycliffe, or since, or hereafter to be set forth, in part or in whole, privily or apertly, upon pain of greater excommunication, until the said translation be allowed by the ordinary of the place, or, if the case so require, by the Council provincial."

For more than a century, that is from the time of

these Constitutions of Arundel in 1408 to that of the Reformation under Henry VIII in 1534, the English Bible given by Wycliffe and his followers remained under interdict, to be read only in secret and with an abiding sense of danger.   Most of our knowledge of what took place in those years, especially the latter portion of them, that is, from 1509 to 1521, comes to us from an unimpeachable source—the registers kept by the bishops themselves.   Two of these stand out prominently, namely, the register of Richard Fitz-james, Bishop of London, and that of John Longland, Bishop of Lincoln.   These records present a curious picture of religious life during the days of our fore-fathers, as well as of the fortunes of the English Bible itself. This is especially true of the county of Buckingham in which Protestant opinions were rife long before the Reformation.   In the days re-ferred to the diocese of Lincoln extended from the Humber to the Thames ; Buckinghamshire therefore was included, and John Longland, the bishop, was especially active in repressing the reading of the Bible in the mother tongue.   Numerous indeed were the indictments for possessing and reading together the Sacred Scriptures with which he dealt. For example we find that John Higgs was summoned because "he had in his custody a book of the Four Evangelists in English and did often read therein"; and Richard Hun because "he hath in his keeping divers English books prohibited and damned by law: as the Apocalypse in English, the Epistles and the Gospels in English, Wycliffe's damnable books, and other books containing infinite errors, in which he hath been a long time accustomed to read, teach, and study daily." James Brewster was charged with having "a certain little book of Scripture in English, of an old writing almost worn for age, whose name is not there expressed." Richard Collins, also, for "having certain English books, as the Gospel of St Luke, the Epistles of St Paul, James and Peter in English, a book of Solomon's in English, and a book called 'The Prick of Conscience.'"

But if it was an ecclesiastical offence to be possessed of a Bible in English or any part thereof, it was a still greater offence for men to meet to read it with their neighbours. The charges under this head are frequent during the years referred to. We read, for example, that Durdant of Iver-court "sitting at dinner with his sons and their wives, after bidding a boy there standing to depart out of the house, that he should not hear and tell, did recite certain places unto them out of the Gospels and the Epistles of St Paul." Ten persons were accused "because that at the marriage of Durdant's daughter they assembled together in a barn and heard a certain Epistle of St Paul read, which reading they well liked." John Butler was compelled because of his oath to detect his three brothers and the mother of Richard Ashford "partly because they were reading two hours together in a certain book of the Acts of the Apostles in English, in Ashford's house." Richard Collins also was detected "who among them was a great reader and had a book of Wycliffe's Wicket, and a book of Luke and one of Paul and a gloss of the Apocalypse." Robert Pope of Amersham "did detect Benet Ward of Beaconsfield because he had given him a book of the Ten Commandments, also the Gospels of Matthew and Mark. Of the same Ward he learned his Christ-cross row and five parts of the eight beatitudes." Certain other persons also were detected for "reading together in the book of the Expositions of the Apocalypse, and communing concerning the matter of the opening of the book with seven clasps."

Manuscript Bibles being scarce and costly, some people exercised their gifts in committing large portions of the Scriptures to memory and reciting them to others. Thomas Chase was detected because James Morden "heard him twice recite the Epistle of St James and the first chapter of St Luke." Agnes Ashford also was charged with teaching this man part of the Sermon on the Mount. "Five times he went to the aforesaid Agnes to learn this lesson... These lessons the said Agnes was bid to recite before six bishops, who straightway enjoined and commanded her that she should teach those lessons

no more to any man, and especially not to her children."
There is a similar record concerning Alice Collins the
wife of Richard Collins. "This Alice was a famous
woman among them, and had a good memory, could
recite much of the Scriptures and other good books;
and therefore when any conventicle of these men did
meet at Burford, commonly she was sent for, to
recite unto them the declaration of the Ten Commandments, and the Epistles of Peter and James."
Her daughter Joan seems to have been quite as
remarkable, "for that she had learned with her father
and mother the Ten Commandments, the seven deadly
sins, the seven works of mercy, the five wits bodily
and ghostly, the eight blessings, and five chapters of
St James's Epistle."

As we go through these records year after year
we find that things which are counted as Christian
excellences now were regarded as ecclesiastical
offences by John Longland, Bishop of Lincoln, and
the penances he enjoined were almost uniform and
all after one condition. Some of the culprits were
sent by him as prisoners to certain abbeys, there to
be kept in perpetual penance and not suffered to pass
the precincts of the monastery. Others were ordered
to stand upon the highest step of the market-cross
on market-days bearing a faggot of wood upon their
shoulder; and on Sunday to stand in the church from
the choir-door going out to the choir-door going in,

and all the time of high mass to hold a faggot of wood upon their shoulders. Also on every Friday during their life to fast on bread and ale only, and on every evening of Corpus Christi during their life to fast on bread and water. As for James Morden and others of the abjurers they were enjoined that for seven years they were to visit the church of Lincoln twice a year from Amersham. But as a pilgrimage from Buckinghamshire to Lincoln cathedral was indeed a serious journey in those days, the sentence was mitigated for some, and they were mercifully permitted to visit the image of our Lady of Missenden for the space of five years instead.

Such was the struggle for light in those far-off days and such the hardships endured by those who went forth in search of the truth of God. Well might John Foxe bear testimony and say that the Church of God in England "hath not lacked great multitudes who tasted and followed the sweetness of God's holy Word almost in as ample manner, for the number of well-disposed hearts as now....Certes the fervent zeal of those Christian days seemed much superior to these our days and times; as manifestly may appear by their sitting up all night in reading and hearing; also by their expenses and charges in buying of books in English, of whom some gave five marks [equal to about £40 in our money], some more, some less, for a book: some gave a load of hay for a few chapters of

St James, or of St Paul in English....To see their travails, their earnest seekings, their burning zeal, their readings, their watchings, their sweet assemblies, their love and concord, their godly living, their faithful demeaning with the faithful, may make us now, in these our days of free profession, to blush for shame."

CHAPTER III

In English Bible translation the next great name after John Wycliffe's is that of William Tyndale. And when we are told that the later version entirely supplanted the earlier, the question arises—Why was this? We have seen that through more than a hundred years Wycliffe's translation rendered noble service to English Christianity—Why then was it superseded? The answer to this question lies on the surface. For one thing, through those hundred years the language had been undergoing a process of serious change, as may be seen at once when Wycliffe's version and Tyndale's are placed side by side. It had come about that the earlier could only with difficulty be understood by the men of the later generation. Then, too, Wycliffe's version had been translated, not from the original Greek in which the New Testament was first written, but from the Latin Vulgate. In other words it was merely a translation from a translation. Wycliffe had no alternative, for even if he had had

3—2

the necessary Greek learning, which he had not, there
were no Greek manuscripts of the New Testament to
be had in England at the time.   For centuries the
only available text of the Scriptures for Europe was
the recension, made by Jerome, of the New Testament largely taken from the Old Latin, and of the
Old Testament from the Greek Septuagint, the one
completed in A.D. 385 and the other in A.D. 405.
Gradually this gained ground through the growing
influence of the Church of Rome and came to be
called the Vulgate or common translation.

But while this was practically the only available
book from which Wycliffe could derive his translation,
within seventy years of his death the situation was
greatly changed.   In 1453 the Greek city of Constantinople was besieged and taken by the Turks.   It
is difficult for us at this distance of time to realise
the terror with which this calamity struck the heart
of Europe.   It seemed like the death-knell of Christen-
dom.   Yet to the Christian Scriptures it worked unexpected gain.   For it brought to Italy the literary
wealth of Greece.   Greek exiles fleeing from Constantinople brought their Greek MSS. and learning
with them.   Nicholas V, thoroughly penetrated with
the spirit of the new learning, seized the opportunity
thus presented.   He eagerly gathered MSS. and employed numerous transcribers and translators within
the Vatican, so that when he died in 1455 he left

behind him a library of 5000 volumes, which before the days of printing was reckoned a vast collection. Twenty-six years later that which is the glory of that great Vatican Library—the *Codex Vaticanus* of the fourth century, the oldest vellum MS. of the Scriptures in existence—was added. Thus MSS. to work from, some of them very ancient, were available for translation as never before.

Then, too, the very year after the Fall of Constantinople the Printing Press with all its possibilities came into existence. That year it passed beyond block-books to movable types, the earliest specimen of printing in this way known being an Indulgence of Nicholas V hearing date November 15, 1454.

The next step in the process of consequence to us now, was the use of MSS. and printing press for the production of the New Testament in Greek. This was the work of Erasmus of Rotterdam, and was produced in 1516 at Basle in connection with Froben, the celebrated printer in that city, a second edition being issued a year or two later. The text of this first printed Greek Testament is of no great critical value, as a text, but it brought to light the important fact that the Vulgate, the Bible of the Church, was not only a translation of a translation, but that in places it was an erroneous document. On this a recent writer has said that "a shock was thus given to the credit of the clergy in the province of literature equal to that which was given in the province of science by the astronomical discoveries of the seventeenth century."

Thus, by successive stages, steps had been taken towards the production of a better Bible, and a Bible in greater numbers than was ever possible by mere hand-writing in the generations before.

Thus the hour had come for a new translation of the Scriptures into the English tongue of the sixteenth century. And with the hour came also the man. That man was William Tyndale. Of his early life we know but little beyond the fact that the evidence is in favour of Melksham Court in the parish of Stinchcombe, in Gloucestershire, being the home of his family, and that he was educated at Oxford where Greek had first begun to be publicly taught in the University by Grocyn and Linacre, on their return from Italy. From 1509 to 1514 Erasmus was Professor of Greek at Cambridge and it has been thought that the fame of his lectures drew Tyndale to that University also about the year 1510. This, however, as Dr Aldis Wright has pointed out, is not now so probable since the discovery of an entry in the Oxford Register which seems to indicate that Tyndale took his M.A. degree in that University in 1515.

What we next know of him is that in 1521 he became tutor in the family of Sir John Walsh at the Manor-house of Old Sodbury in Gloucestershire. At

Sir John's table there went forward many a brisk
argument between the tutor and "divers great beneficed men, as abbots, deans, archdeacons and other
divers doctors and learned men." As they varied in
opinion and judgment Tyndale would show them on
the book the places by open and manifest Scripture,
a process which to them proved distasteful, and "in
the continuance thereof these beneficed doctors
waxed weary and bare a secret grudge in their hearts
against Master Tyndale." On a day long remembered, one of them being sore pressed in argument
said—"We were better without God's law than the
Pope's." Whereupon Tyndale defied the Pope and
all his works, and, looking earnestly at his opponent,
went on to say—"If God spare my life, ere many
years I will cause a boy that driveth the plough
shall know more of the Scriptures than thou doest."
It may be that in this utterance of his Tyndale had
in mind the vivid words which Erasmus had written
in the preface to that Greek Testament of 1516 he
had come to know. "I would," said Erasmus, "that
all private women should read the Gospel and Paul's
Epistles. And I wish that they were translated into
all languages that they may be read and known, not
only by the Scotch and Irish, but also by the Turks
and Saracens. Let it be that many would smile, yet
some would receive it. I would that the husbandman at the plough should sing something from hence,

that the weaver at his loom should sing something
from hence, that the traveller might beguile the
weariness of his journey by narrations of this kind."
Thus one living word spoken leads to another, and
living words to living deeds. Tyndale had come to
think that there is no security for the permanent
spiritual enlightenment of a people except their
natural intelligence is guided by the revealed truth of
God. "Which thing," says he, "only moved me to translate the New Testament. Because I had perceived
by experience how it was impossible to establish the
lay people in any truth except the Scriptures were
plainly laid before them in their mother tongue, that
they might see the process, order and meaning of the
text; for else, whatsoever truth is taught them, these
enemies of all truth quench it again."

It is clear that the production of a Bible in the
changed English of his time had become something
of a purpose in Tyndale's mind. But he soon found
that in Gloucestershire there was neither the necessary quiet nor freedom and he determined to make his
way to London and secure the help of Tonstal the
bishop, for he had heard Erasmus praise him exceedingly for his great learning. But he met with but a
cold reception when he applied for a place in his
lordship's service. The bishop had more he said
than he could well sustain and he advised Tyndale to
seek somewhere else in London. So he lingered on

with hope deferred nearly a year but " understood at the last not only that there was no room in my Lord of London's palace, to translate the New Testament, but also that there was no place to do it in all England, as experience doth now openly declare." This was written in a preface to the book of Genesis which he issued in 1530 and describes his state of mind in 1524.

Resolving to leave England Tyndale sailed over to Hamburg in the month of May, and appears to have been in the same city in the early spring of the following year, during which time he was engaged in the work of translation. Later, in 1525, we find him in Cologne where his New Testament was being secretly printed at the press of Peter Quentel. Three thousand copies of the first ten sheets (A—K) had been printed off when the secret oozed out through the intervention of Johann Dobneck, better known as Cochlaeus. This man was living in exile in Cologne and being engaged in literary labours he became intimate with the printers of the city, and learnt from them in their cups that there was something going on, of which they knew, which would soon turn England Lutheran. The expense, they said, was being met by English merchants who had engaged to convey the work over into England and spread it widely in the country. On finding out this secret Cochlaeus lost no time in revealing the plot to Hermann Rinck, a nobleman of Cologne, well known to Henry VIII and the Emperor Charles V, and he having satisfied himself of the truth of this report applied to the senate and obtained an interdict of the work. Finding that their secret was out Tyndale and his assistant, William Roye, fled up the Rhine, with all the haste they could, to the city of Worms, carrying the 3000 copies of the first ten sheets of the book with them. What became of that first edition, printed in quarto, whether it was completed or not, is not quite clear. The probability is that it was, 3000 copies being printed at Worms by Peter Schoeffer in 1525. But before it was completed Tyndale changed his plan and commenced to print an octavo edition of his New Testament, the quarto edition being completed after the printing of this. Of that first quarto edition a precious fragment was discovered in 1834, containing the prologue and the Gospel of Matthew as far as the 22nd chapter. It is now in the Grenville Library of the British Museum, No. 12,179, and consists of 21 leaves going to the end of sheet H, and ending with the words, "Friend, how camest thou in hither, and" (Matt. xxii. 12). It has been photo-lithographed with an introduction by Mr Arber. Of the octavo edition printed at Worms by Peter Schoeffer (1525–6) only two copies are known to be in existence. One of these is preserved in the library of the Baptist College at Bristol; it wants the title-page and prologue, probably about eight leaves. The other is in St Paul's Cathedral Library, wanting probably 78 leaves. There is a lithographed reproduction in the Ryland's Library, one of six copies printed on vellum, made from the Bristol copy by Francis Fry in 1862. The Cathedral copy, lent by the Dean and Chapter for the purpose, was shown in the Caxton Exhibition of 1877.

The Testaments reached England some time in the spring of 1526, and everything possible was done to prevent the entrance of the forbidden books and to destroy those which did come in. Many copies were bought up for large sums of money, but this was futile work in the way of destruction for the money thus obtained only set more printers at work, and we find that as many as three pirated editions were issued by Antwerp printers in 1526 and the two following years. This English New Testament was the great event of the time. It found its way into England in corn-ships and bales of merchandise and was mysteriously carried into the country far and near. One of the most active agents in their distribution was Simon Fish, author of the "Supplicacyon for the Beggars," then living near the White Friars. The Bishop of St Asaph seems to have been the first to call Cardinal Wolsey's attention to the contraband trade thus being carried on. The Cardinal, however, was disposed to make light of the matter, but the

Bishop of London was urgent that steps should be taken to arrest the movement, and orders were given that the books should be burnt wherever found. To make the condemnation the more impressive it was further ordered that there should be a public burning in St Paul's Cathedral to follow a sermon by the Bishop of Rochester at Paul's Cross. On the 4th of May 1530, accordingly, a procession was formed from the Fleet prison to the Cathedral. The warden of the Fleet was there, and the knight-marshal, and the tipstaffs, and "all the company they could make," with "bills and glaives." In the midst of these officials there marched six men in penitential dresses bearing faggots and lighted tapers. The Cathedral was already crowded when they arrived and Cardinal Wolsey, supported on each side by bishops, priors, abbots, chaplains and spiritual doctors, sat enthroned in the nave on a raised platform. Opposite the platform over the north door was the far-famed Rood of Northen, and at the foot of the rood, inside the rail, a fire was burning, and round the fire were several baskets filled with New Testaments. The signal being given the knight-marshal led the six prisoners three times round the blazing pile, they casting in more faggots as they passed. Then the Testaments were heaped on the top of the faggots and went up in flame.

Nor was this the only scene of the kind in those

troubled days, as Foxe, in vivid narrative, has told us. Among those who received Tyndale's Testaments in England was Thomas Garret, Curate of All Hallows, Cheapside. Wolsey searched for him "in all London" but found he had "gone to Oxford to make sale of the books to such as he knew to be lovers of the Gospel." He was apprehended but escaping from custody made his way to his friend Anthony Dalaber who has told us the story. "With deep sighs and plenty of tears he prayed me," Dalaber writes, "to help to convey him away, and so he cast off his hood and his gown wherein he came to me and desired me to give him a coat with sleeves" that thus disguised he might make his way to Germany. "Then kneeled we both down together on our knees, lifting up our hearts to God, our heavenly Father, desiring him with plenty of tears so to conduct and prosper him in his journey that he might well escape the danger of his enemies. And then we embraced and kissed one the other...and so he departed. When he was gone I straightway did shut my chamber-door and went into my study and took the New Testament in my hands, kneeled down on my knees and with many a deep sigh and salt tear, I did with much deliberation read over the tenth chapter of Matthew's Gospel, and when I had so done with fervent prayer I did commit unto God our dearly beloved brother Garret, and also that he would endue his tender and lately born little flock in Oxford with heavenly strength." But Garret was seized and brought back to Oxford. Then search went on and discoveries were made of hidden books even in Cardinal Wolsey's own College. And it turned out that the "lately born flock" was not equal to the strain. The hidden books were collected, a great fire was publicly kindled at Carfax, and Garret and Dalaber with others, who in after-days were to take part in the Reformation, were compelled as part of their penance to cast the gathered books into the fire. Such was the fate of Tyndale's New Testaments when first introduced into his own University of Oxford.

Meantime, while all this was going on at home, Tyndale himself was at work abroad, bent on producing a translation of the Old Testament as well as the New. Devoting himself to the study of Hebrew he went in 1527 to Marburg in Hesse where he published his two most important controversial works, and what more concerns us here is, he also published the first part of the Old Testament in English. Early in 1530 he sent forth his version of the Pentateuch made direct from the original Hebrew with the aid of Luther's German version. Some parts of this work were printed in black letter and others in Roman type, and the book is memorable as being the first part of the Old Testament ever printed in English. It has been said of this little volume that it ranks second only to the New Testament of 1525, and is no less important as a monument of the English language, and as the basis of all subsequent English versions. The colophon at the end of Genesis alone gives name and place of printer, and reads thus : "Emprented at Marlborow [*Anglicé* Marburg] in the lande of Hesse by me Hans Luft, the yere of oure Lorde Mccccexxx the xvij dayes of Januarij." On the margin of Numbers xxxii. 18 —"How shall I curse whom God cursed not," Tyndale printed the well-known comment—"The Pope can tell howe." Several copies of this version of the Pentateuch are in existence, but only one, the one in the Grenville Library, in perfect condition. There was a second edition in 1534. In 1531 Tyndale printed at Antwerp his translation of the book of Jonab to which he appended an interesting prologue. A unique copy of this long-lost work, which was discovered in 1861 by Lord Arthur Hervey, is now in the British Museum. From 1533, if not earlier, till his arrest in 1535, Tyndale resided in Antwerp where in November, 1534, he published the first revision of his Testament in octavo. In this revised edition there is a prologue to the Epistle to the Romans extending to 34 pages, which though only appearing now had been written in 1526 after the issue of the first edition. This prologue was also printed in a separate form, the only surviving copy being found in the Bodleian Library. Two other revisions also of the octavo edition of his Testament were made in 1535 and 1536 by Tyndale himself. The first of these is entitled—"The Newe Testament dylygently corrected and compared with the Greke by Willyam Tindale and finesshed in the yere of our Lord God AMD and xxxv." No mention is made of place or printer, but it is thought to be from the press of Hans van Ruremonde at Antwerp. The last revision is also in octavo and bears as a printer's mark the two letters G H, which the late Henry Bradshaw recognised as the initials of the Antwerp publisher Godfried van der Haghen. The printer he frequently employed was Martin Emperour [= de Keyser], who was probably therefore the printer of this last revision.

The years of Tyndale's life at Antwerp were years of great literary activity. It was here he published a revision of his translation of the Pentateuch, with a new preface, some changes being made in the book of Genesis. Even during his imprisonment of sixteen months in the fortress of Vilvorde, which commenced in May 1535, he was by no means idle. In a touching letter to the Governor, the Marquis of Bergen-op-Zoom, in which he petitioned for warmer clothing, he asked also for a Hebrew Bible, grammar and dictionary. It is conjectured also that during this same imprisonment he finished a translation of the books of the Old Testament from Joshua to

Heſe be the wordes which Moſes ſpake vn to all Iſrael, on the other ſyde Iordayne in the wildErneſſe and in the feldes by the red ſee, betwene Pharã ãd Tophel, Laban, Haze roth and Dilahab. xij. dayes iurney from Horeb vnto Cades bernea , by the waye that leadeth vnto mount Seir. And it fortuned the firſt daye of the. xi. moneth in the fortieth yere, that Moſes ſpake vnto the childern of Iſrael acordinge vnto all that the Lorde had geuen him in commaundment vnto them, after that he had ſmote Sihon the kynge of the Amorites which dwelt in Heſbon, and Og kinge of Baſan which dwelt at Aſtaroth in Edrei.

On the other ſyde Iordayne in the londe of Moab, Moſes begane to declare this lawe ſaynge: the Lorde oure God ſpake vnto us in Horeb ſayenge: Ye haue dwelt longe ynough in this mount: departe therfore and take youe te iurney and goo vnto the hilles of the Amo rites and vnto all places nye there vnto: both feldes, hilles and dales: and vnto the ſouth and vnto the ſees ſyde in the londe of Canaan, and vnto libanon: euen vnto the greate ryuer Eu

B phrates

Second Chronicles inclusive.   There is good reason
also for thinking that this part of his work re-
appeared in " Matthew's " Bible of 1537 ; and it has
been said that "Matthew" is a pseudonym, and
perhaps stands for John Rogers, Tyndale's friend.

So far as the original text was concerned he was
limited to the Greek Testament of 1516.   The MSS.
Erasmus used for that, five in number, are still at
Basle, and not one of them is ancient, the most
valuable of the five being one written in the 10th
century; that followed entirely in the translation of
the Gospels was one written as late as the 15th
century.   But while Tyndale, no more than other
men, could go before his time in such matters, to
him, as Dr Westcott has truly said, more than to
any other man it has been allowed to give its
characteristic shape to our English Bible.   To the
same purport the compilers of the valuable Historical
Catalogue of the Bible Society have noted it as
"remarkable to what an extent the first printed
English Testament fixed the phraseology of all its
successors.   Even in the Revised Version of 1881 it
has been calculated that at least eighty per cent.
of the words stand precisely as they stood in Tyndale's
Testament of 1525."   It has also been noted as
matter for surprise that there is so little difference
between the English of 1525 and that of the ordinary
Bibles.   For in the Gospel of Mark and the Epistle

B.   4

to the Hebrews there are not more than eighty words which are not found in the Authorised Version of 1611, that is, there are not more than four strangers in every thousand words. Sometimes a change made from Tyndale was a change decidedly for the worse, as in the case of St John x. 16 where "there shall be one *flock*" was altered to "one *fold*," a change which has been set right in the Revised Version of 1881. No doubt changes which have been improvements have been made by those who followed Tyndale; but the plan and spirit of the work are his. To him men are indebted more than they realise for melodious phrases and happy turns of expression, such as: "singing and making melody in your hearts"; "in Him we live and move and have our being"; "turned to flight the armies of the aliens." In his account of the production of the English Bible Froude the historian is inaccurate in his details, but he expresses the calm judgment of those who know when he speaks as follows: "Of the translation itself, though since that time it has been many times revised and altered, we may say that it is substantially the Bible with which we are familiar. The peculiar genius—if such a word may be permitted—which breathes through it—the mingled tenderness and majesty—the Saxon simplicity—the preternatural grandeur—unequalled, unapproached in the attempted improvements of modern scholars—all are here, and bear the impress of the mind of one man—William Tyndale. Lying, while engaged in that great office, under the shadow of death, the sword above his head and ready at any moment to fall, he worked under circumstances alone perhaps truly worthy of the task which was laid upon him—his spirit, as it were divorced from the world, moved in a purer element than common air."

While living at Antwerp Tyndale lodged in the house of Thomas Poyntz, an Englishman who kept there a house of English merchants. An informer of the name of Philips, having satisfied himself of Tyndale's identity, betrayed him to the authorities at Brussels, and so he came within the jurisdiction of the Emperor Charles V. Arrested in the spring of 1535 and taken to the fortress-prison of Vilvorde he remained in captivity nearly a year and a half. Then in the October of 1536 his case came up for judgment at the Augsburg Assembly, and there by virtue of the Emperor's decree he was condemned to die. On Friday the 6th of October, after seventeen months imprisonment, he was led to the scaffold where he was first strangled and then burnt. Like many who have lived to serve their generation, for sixteen years, during which he had plied his work, he had gone through sorrowful experiences. In modest, manly way, and speaking only in self-defence, he refers to

4—2

these : "My pains therein taken, my poverty, my exile out of mine own natural country, and bitter absence from my friends ; my hunger, my thirst, my cold, the great danger wherewith I am everywhere encompassed, and finally, other hard and sharp fighting, I endured by reason that I hoped with my labours to do honour to God, true service to my Prince, and pleasure to his Commons." But now his *via dolorosa* had come to its end, and his prayer, like that of his Master, was for those who had wronged him. His last thought was for the fatherland he had left so long and loved so well. "Lord !" cried he, "open the King of England's eyes."

CHAPTER IV

COVERDALE'S BIBLE AND THE GREAT BIBLE

DURING the seventy-five years between the last issue of Tyndale's Testaments and the publication of the Authorised Version of 1611, six different versions of the English Bible issued from the press, and in saying this we are not taking account of the Rheims-Douai Bible, the Roman Catholic English Version dating between 1582 and 1610. These six versions were: Coverdale's Bible of 1535; "Matthew's" Bible of 1537; Taverner's Bible of 1539; the Great Bible, also of 1539; the Geneva Bible of 1560; and the Bishops' Bible of 1568. It will be in the memory of our readers that when Coverdale appeared upon the scene Tyndale's Bible was far from complete. The New Testament had been finished and several times revised; the book of Jonah had been translated separately; and the Pentateuch had been issued in a revised second edition. Probably also a translation of the Old Testament from Joshua to Second Chronicles had been made by Tyndale and left in manuscript. This being the extent to which his work had gone it will be seen at once that a large portion of Scripture, including the Psalter and the Prophetical Books, still remained untranslated.

It is here that Miles Coverdale's work comes in and fills an important place. This man was a native of the North Riding of Yorkshire, where he was born in 1488, and we know of him further that he was Bishop of Exeter in 1551. Foxe tells us that Coverdale met Tyndale by appointment at Hamburg in 1529, and from Easter till December in that year helped him in translating the five books of Moses, so that there was so far a close and friendly relation existing between them.

It would seem that he set about completing Tyndale's work, being urged thereto and commissioned by others. These are his words : "To say the truth before God, it was neither my labour nor desire to have this work put in my hand, nevertheless it grieved me that other nations should be more plenteously provided for with the Scripture in their mother-tongue than we ; therefore when I was instantly required, though I could not do so well as I would, I thought it yet my duty to do my best and that with a good will."

Coverdale made no claim to be a direct translator from the original Hebrew, but to have made his version from German and Latin sources. He trans-

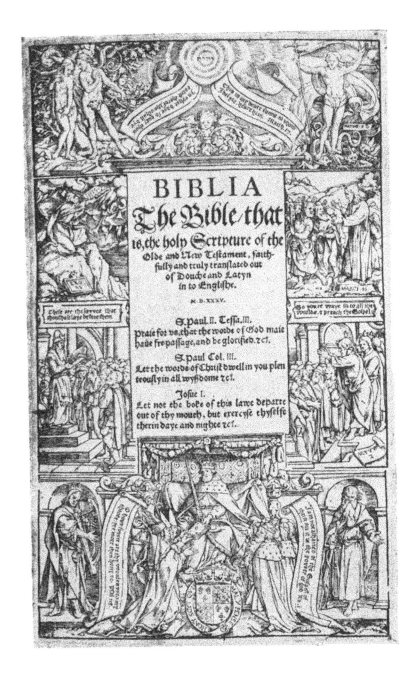

COVERDALE'S BIBLE

From Mr W. Aldis Wright's copy

lated he says out of "five interpreters." He had some
knowledge of Hebrew to help him to discriminate
between various renderings, but in the main his version is based on the Swiss-German version of Zwingli
and Leo Juda (1542–9), known as the Zurich Bible,
and on the Latin of Pagninus. So far as the Pentateuch is concerned, his translation has been described
as the Zurich translation rendered into English by
the help of Tyndale with constant reference to Luther,
Pagninus and the Vulgate. It will be seen that
Tyndale was a great resource to him when we find
that in the whole Epistle of St James containing
108 verses, there is only a difference of three words
between them.

Still, notwithstanding this dependence upon others,
the value of Coverdale's version will be felt at once
when we consider that for three-fourths of the Old
Testament this is the first printed English Bible, and
as such still stands alone, inasmuch as it had great
influence in the shaping of the Authorised Version
of 1611. His Bible is divided into six parts, the fifth
part containing the Apocryphal books arranged in
the same order as that of the Authorised Version;
and the sixth part consisting of the books of the New
Testament arranged in the same order as in Luther
and Tyndale's version, that is, the Epistles of St
Peter and St John come in before and not after the
Epistle to the Hebrews. The most characteristic

portion of Coverdale's translation is that of the
Psalter, and this still remains in use as being the one
printed in the Book of Common Prayer.   While in
the revision of this book in 1662 the Gospels, Epistles
and other portions of Scripture were taken from the
Authorised Version, the Psalms as translated by
Coverdale were retained as being smoother and more
amenable to musical treatment.   In the Authorised
Version, too, many of the renderings most valued for
their beauty and tenderness are his ; such as : "My
heart and flesh faileth, but God is the strength of my
heart, and my portion for ever"; "Enter not into
judgment with thy servant, for in thy sight shall no
man living be justified"; "Cast me not away from
thy presence, and take not thy Holy Spirit from me";
"For thy loving-kindness is better than life ; my lips
shall praise thee"; "Thou Lord in the beginning
hast laid the foundation of the earth, and the heavens
are the work of thy hands.   They shall perish but
thou shalt endure : they shall all wax old as doth a
garment ; and as a vesture shalt thou change them,
and they shall be changed.   But thou art the same and
thy years shall not fail."   We feel there is a certain
majesty about these passages entitling Coverdale to a
high place in our literature.

The relation of this Bible of his to the civil power
seems fitful and uncertain.   In 1535 it was printed
out of the country by Froschover of Zurich and was

dedicated to the King, but appeared without express license. The following year it was printed at home by Nycolson of Southwark but again without royal license. Then again in 1538 another edition was printed by Nycolson and this time the title-page proclaims the fact that it was "Set forth wyth the Kynges moost gracious licence." The explanation of the difference is to be found in the fact that during these years the rupture with Rome had become an accomplished fact. Wolsey had fallen and Thomas Cromwell had become the King's Vicegerent in all causes ecclesiastical, with precedence over all prelates and peers. In the issue of the First Royal Injunctions of 1536 we have the first act of pure supremacy on the part of the King in the affairs of the Church, and in them we find him urging the clergy to give themselves to the study of Holy Scripture. But the changing attitude of the Crown to the Bible is brought out more clearly in the scene which took place at a Council of Convocation held in 1537. Foxe, making use of a narrative given to him by Alesius, or Hales, has described it for us. As Cromwell entered, the bishops and prelates rose up and did obeisance to him as their Vicar-General, he in turn saluting them, and then seating himself in the highest place at the table. Presently he proceeded to address them, setting forth the purpose for which they were met, and telling them that the King's desire was that they would conclude all things by the Word of God. His Majesty, he said, would not suffer the Scriptures to be wrested or defaced by any papistical laws, or any authority of doctors or councils, much less would he admit any articles or doctrines not contained in the Scriptures. In reply the bishops gave thanks unto the King's Majesty for his zeal and his most godly exhortation. But controversy arose at once when Stokesley, Bishop of London, maintained the validity of the Seven Sacraments, the Archbishop of Canterbury going one way with his followers, and the Archbishop of York another, with those who agreed with him. The question was really one of final authority; where does it rest, with the Church or the Bible? Foxe, the Bishop of Hereford, contended for the Bible, for the light of the Gospel hath put to flight all misty darkness, and it will be supreme "though we resist in vain ever so much." In spite of opposition that book was making its way, he said. "The lay people do now know the Holy Scripture better than many of us; and the Germans have made the text of the Bible so plain and easy, by the Hebrew and Greek tongues, that now many things may be better understood without any glosses at all, than by all the commentaries of the doctors." He urged them not to deceive themselves by the hope that there was nothing which the power and authority of the pope could not

quench in process of time, but rather to take the
other view "that there is nothing so feeble and weak,
so that it be true but it shall find place, and be able
to stand against all falsehood." He concluded with
these eloquent words: "Truth is the daughter of
Time and Time is the mother of Truth; and whatsoever is besieged of Truth cannot long continue;
and upon whose side Truth doth stand, that ought
not to be thought transitory or that it will ever fall.
All things consist not in painted eloquence, and
strength or authority: for the Truth is of so great
power, strength and efficacy that it can neither be
defended with words, nor be overcome with any
strength, but after she hath hidden herself long, at
length she putteth up her head and appeareth."
This noble utterance may well coincide with the appearance of that first completed and printed English
Bible which Coverdale sent forth; and it may well
stand as fitting watchword at the opening of that
new era in the history of that Bible which was even
now at the doors.

The year 1537 which saw a new edition of Coverdale's Bible "overseen and corrected," saw also the
issue of another Bible described as "*Matthew's*,"
about which there is a certain air of mystery. It
was printed in black letter, in double columns, the
title-page sets forth that it was "truly and purely
translated into English by Thomas Matthew" and at

foot of that page it was said to be set forth "with the Kynge's most gracious lycence." It seems to be generally agreed that the name of Matthew was assumed by John Rogers, an intimate friend of Tyndale, an earnest Protestant and one of the martyrs of Mary's time. The version bearing this name is of a composite character and comprised a reprint of Tyndale's New Testament and his Penta-teuch. From Ezra to the end of the Apocrypha, not excluding Jonah, it is substantially Coverdale's version; but from Joshua to Chronicles the text differs so widely from Coverdale, that it is supposed to be from the translations left behind him by Tyndale. It was furnished with a dedication to the King and Queen, and the expense of the work, probably printed at Antwerp, was defrayed by two London citizens, R. Grafton and E. Whitchurch. The first news of its appearance in England is contained in a letter from Cranmer to Cromwell. "My especial good lord," he writes, "these shall be to signify unto the same that you shall receive by the bringer thereof a bible in English, both of a new translation and of a new print...which in mine opinion is very well done, and therefore I pray your lordship to read the same. And as for the translation, so far as I have read thereof, I like it better than any other translation heretofore made....I pray you, my Lord, that you will exhibit the book unto the King's highness, and to obtain of his grace, if you can, a license that the same may be sold and read of every person, without danger of any act, proclamation or ordinance to the contrary, until such time that we bishops shall set forth a better translation which I think will not be till a day after doomsday." Cromwell did as Cranmer desired and presently informed him that he had not only shown the Bible to the King but had also "obtained of his grace that the same shall be allowed by his authority to be bought and read within this nation." Dr Westcott points out the deep significance of what had thus been accomplished : "By Cranmer's petition, by Cromwell's influence and by Henry's authority, without any formal ecclesiastical decision, the book was given to the English people, which is the foundation of the text of our present Bible. From Matthew's Bible—itself a combination of the labours of Tyndale and Coverdale—all later revisions have been successively formed. In that the general character and mould of our whole version was definitely fixed. The labours of the next seventy-five years were devoted to improving it in detail."

It may now be mentioned in passing, though the matter is of small importance, that the successful sale of Matthew's Bible led in 1539 to the issuing of a rival edition, as a private venture, by "John Byddell for Thomas Barthlet" with Richard Taverner

as editor.   From the name of the editor it is known
as *Taverner's Bible*.   He was a Cambridge man and
was also for a year and a half a student at Oxford.
About 1530 he became a member of the Inner Temple;
he afterwards went to Court and through Cromwell's
influence became one of the Clerks of the Signet.   In
1539 his version of the Bible was printed at the Sign
of the Sun in Fleet Street, London, and was allowed
to be publicly read in churches.   The influence of
the Vulgate is clearly traceable in what changes he
made, which were but small in the Old Testament,
but more numerous in the New.   Those who have
examined the book report that it is evidently the
work of a scholar, but of a scholar of capricious and
uncertain cast of mind.   His version was once afterwards reprinted in its entirety but had little influence
in after years.

We come now to the important version known as
The Great Bible—"the hole byble of the largyest
volume," which came out in 1539.   This is the book
referred to in the Second Royal Injunctions of 1538,
sent to Cranmer by Cromwell under date September
30.   In section 2 the following order was issued to
the clergy: "You shall provide on this side the feast
of Easter next coming, one book of the whole Bible
of the largest volume, in English, and the same set
up in some convenient place within the said church
that you have cure of, whereas your parishioners may

most commodiously resort to the same and read it; the charges of which book shall be rateably borne between you, the parson, and the parishioners aforesaid." In section 3 the clergy are charged—"You shall discourage no man privily or apertly from the reading or hearing of the said Bible, but shall expressly provoke, stir, and exhort every person to read the same, as that which is the very lively word of God, that every Christian man is bound to embrace, believe and follow, if he look to be saved."

The Bible, thus for the first time in English history to be openly placed in the churches for any man to read who could, was practically a revision of Matthew's Bible carried out by Coverdale himself. About the same time that Coverdale's own Bible of 1535 was going through the press there was being prepared a new Latin version of the Old Testament, giving also the Hebrew text and a commentary chiefly from Hebrew sources, the work of Sebastian Münster of Basle. It was, of course, not available at the time Coverdale was at work and he had to content himself with the Zurich version, but when he came afterwards to compare the two he felt at once that Münster's version was greatly superior as a text to work from. It was therefore adopted and the Great Bible is really the text of Matthew taken as a basis and revised by the help of Münster. This refers to the Old Testament only, but a revision of the New Testament was carried out also on similar principles and what Münster's version, as a text, was for the Old Testament that of Erasmus was for the New. But next to Erasmus the Complutensian edition was most largely made use of in what changes were made in the revision.

The Great Bible thus constituted was arranged in the first instance to be printed in Paris, that city taking precedence at that time in the matters of paper, types and workmanship. Through Cromwell's influence a licence was obtained from Francis I, the King of France, by which Coverdale and Grafton were authorised to print and transmit to England the Latin or the English Bible, it being a condition that no private or unlawful opinions should be introduced, and that all dues and obligations should be properly discharged. So the execution of the work was entrusted to Francis Regnault, a Paris printer of high reputation, and commenced on a splendid scale; Coverdale and Grafton going over to superintend. By September Cromwell was informed by Coverdale that in about four months he hoped the printing would be complete. Still they were not without misgivings as to possible interference and in December their fears were verified, for in that month an Order came from the Inquisitor General for France, forbidding further progress and ordering the removal of the sheets. Fortunately some of the sheets had been sent on to England and so were safe. And even those that were seized by the authorities, "four great dry vats-full," were afterwards re-purchased from a haberdasher, to whom they had been sold as wastepaper. And the work was not really stopped but only delayed. For Cromwell, a man of executive ability, at once arranged that both types and presses and printers should be brought over to England and the work completed there. In this way the Great Bible which Cromwell in the Injunctions of 1538 had ordered beforehand to be placed in the churches by Easter, was really issued in April 1539. The title-page describes it as "The Byble in Englysh, that is to say the content of all the holy scrypture both of y⁰ Olde and Newe testamente truly translated after the veryte of the Hebrue and Greke textes by y⁰ dylygent studye of dyverse excellent, learned men expert in the forsayde tonges. Prynted by Rychard Grafton and Edward Whitchurch. 1539." A fine copy printed on vellum and illuminated, which was originally prepared for Thomas Cromwell himself, as the great promoter of the enterprise, is preserved in the Library of St John's College, Cambridge.

The Great Bible is sometimes called Cranmer's Bible; this is a mistake, however, as he seems to have had no connection with the enterprise till the appearance of the *second* edition in April 1540. For this he wrote a prologue which appeared in subsequent editions.   The first title has these words: "This is the Byble apoynted to the use of the Churches." Of this edition the British Museum possesses a fine copy, printed on vellum and illuminated, which was presented to Henry VIII by Anthony Marler, of London, haberdasher, who is said to have borne the expense of these editions.   The *third* Great Bible came out in July 1540, and the *fourth* in November of the same year.   In April 1541 Anthony Marler received permission to sell copies of the Great Bible unbound for ten shillings sterling, and bound, "being trimmed with bullyons," for twelve shillings, equivalent, it has been calculated, to about £6 and £7. 5s. 0d. of present value.   The following month appeared the *fifth* Great Bible; in November of the same year the *sixth*; and in December the *seventh* and last of the 1539–41 series, being the sixth with Cranmer's prologue.

All these editions, though appointed to be read in churches, unlike the Authorised Version of 1611 have no dedication.   The title-page takes a pictorial form said to have been designed by Hans Holbein, in the upper part of which the Lord Christ is represented in the clouds of heaven; lower down the King appears on his throne handing the Word of God to the bishops and clergy on the right and to Cromwell and others of the laity on his left.   There was no mere courtly flattery in thus representing the Bible as being now accessible to the people.   For copies were now

THE GREAT BIBLE: 1539

From Mr W. Aldis Wright's copy

actually within reach in their churches. Even Bishop Bonner, unhappily so prominent in the persecution of Bible-reading men in the days of Mary, actually "set up Six Bibles in certain convenient places of St Paul's Church," after the proclamation of May 1540 ; adding a pious admonition to the readers to bring with them "discretion, honest intent, charity, reverence and quiet behaviour." So far as the facts have come down to us, it is clear the people were not slow to take advantage of the opportunity thus afforded to them. Strype, the historian, making use of a manuscript of Foxe tells us : "It was wonderful to see with what joy the book of God was received not only among the learneder sort and those that were noted for lovers of the reformation, but generally all England over among all the vulgar and common people ; and with what greediness God's word was read and what resort to places where the reading of it was. Everybody that could bought the book or busily read it or got others to read it to them if they could not themselves, and divers more elderly people learned to read on purpose." Foxe further relates how at the beginning of the reign of Elizabeth he met a certain William Maldon who could remember that "when the King had allowed the Bible to be set forth to be read in all the churches immediately several poor men in the town of Chelmsford in Essex, where his father lived and where he was born, bought the New Testament and on Sundays sat reading of it in the lower end of the church : many would flock about them to hear their reading ; and he among the rest, being then but fifteen years old, came every Sunday to hear the glad tidings of the Gospel."

It is strange to find that this flood-tide of interest in the Scripture should so soon have been followed by a time of suspense and reaction as we find it was. The explanation is to be found in the political changes of the time. After a period of masterful power Thomas Cromwell had fallen from the royal favour as Cardinal Wolsey had fallen before him. He was assailed by his opponents, an Act of Attainder passed against him without a dissentient, and on the 28th of July 1540 he was beheaded on Tower Hill. Those who had been in opposition before, now came into power and favour in the Council with Gardiner at their head. These were conservatives of the Old Roman faith and hostile to the Reformation. They were, therefore, not slow to take advantage of the change. In 1543 an Act was passed prohibiting the use of Tyndale's translation, and ordering that all notes and marginal commentaries in other copies should be obliterated. It further provided that no woman (unless she be a noble or gentlewoman), and that no artificer, journeyman, servant husbandman or labourer under the degree of yeoman should read or use any part of the Bible under pain of fines and imprisonment. Further, in 1546 a proclamation was issued by which Coverdale's version as well as Tyndale's was expressly prohibited, the effect being that the Great Bible was now the only translation not interdicted. On all sides the Bibles proscribed were sought out and destroyed. Thus this time of reaction brought sorrow to many. But it was not to be for long. It came to an end with the King's life, and the year after his proclamation of prohibition, on the 28th of January 1547, Henry VIII passed out of this world, leaving other actors to come on to the stage, and other scenes to follow.

CHAPTER V

THREE RIVAL VERSIONS

WITH the Accession of Edward VI in January 1547 a change for the better came over the fortunes of the English Bible. The restrictions placed upon the printing and reading of the Scriptures were at once removed, and in the first year of the new reign an Injunction was issued requiring every beneficed person to provide within three months a copy of the English Bible "of the largest volume"; and within twelve months a copy of the "Paraphrase on the Gospels" by Erasmus, these to be set up in some convenient place in the church where they might be read by the parishioners. This English version of the Latin paraphrase or commentary of Erasmus was "Enprinted at London in Flete-strete at the signe of the Sunne, by Edward Whitchurche the last day of Januarie 1548." Several translators were employed in its preparation, Miles Coverdale, John Olde, Nicholas Udall and others; and curious to relate, the Princess Mary, afterwards Queen Mary, herself translated the greater part of the paraphrase upon St John's Gospel. As this work was required to be placed in the churches within a twelvemonth, several presses were engaged upon it, with the result that Dr W. Aldis Wright found no fewer than six varieties of the Paraphrase in existence. Among the incidents of the time it is mentioned that in 1548 the churchwardens of St Margaret's, Westminster, paid five shillings for the half-part of the work ; and in 1549 those of Wigtoft in Lincolnshire seven shillings for the whole, and for a chain to fasten it, fourpence. From the same printing offiee in Fleet Street there had been issued the previous year the earliest edition of the Scriptures in Edward's reign, the only issue in 1547. It bore the title, "The Newe Testament in Englyshe according to the translacion of the Great Byble." It was followed by many more. Short as Edward's reign was no fewer than forty editions either of the whole Bible or of the New Testament issued from the press.

During this reign also there was produced a fragment of a version of the New Testament containing the Gospel of Matthew and the first chapter of Mark, which may be mentioned in passing as one of the curiosities of the time. It was the work of Sir John Cheke, Professor of Greek in the University of Cambridge, who had been also tutor to the King when Prince Edward. Milton says he " taught Cambridge and King Edward Greek." The manuscript, which has unfortunately lost a leaf, is preserved in the Library of Corpus Christi College, Cambridge. It is in Cheke's beautiful handwriting, and though probably made in 1550 was not published till it was edited by the Rev. James Goodwin in 1843. Its special characteristic seems to have been an attempt to express the ideas of the original in home-born words and the language of the common people rather than in the semi-Latin then much in vogue. It may perhaps be described as an anticipation in the 16th century of what is known as the "Twentieth Century Bible" of our own times. One or two extracts may show the kind of thing aimed at: "When Jesus was born in Bethlehem, a city of Jewry in King Herod's days, lo, then the wizards came from the East parts to Jerusalem, and asked where the King of Jews was that was new born"; "Come to me all that labour and be burdened and I will ease you. Take my yoke on you and learn of me, for I am mild and of a lowly heart. And ye shall find quietness for yourselves"; "And his disciples seeing him walking on the sea were troubled, saying that it was a phantasm, and they cried out for fear. Jesus bye and bye spake to them and said, Be of good cheer. It is I, fear not. Peter answered unto him, Sir, saith he, If it be thou, bid me come on the water unto thee. And he said, Come on. And Peter came down out of the boat and walked on the waters to come to Jesus. And seeing the wind strong, was afeard, and when he began to sink he cried out."

With the death of Edward VI, and the Accession of Queen Mary, came change amounting to revolution. At once the public reading of the Scripture was prohibited, a proclamation of June 1555 denounced the writings of Tyndale, Frith, Cranmer and Coverdale, and during these five years there was neither Bible nor Testament published in the realm.

But Mary's policy of repression led indirectly to the production of that *Genevan* version of the Scriptures which Dr Westcott describes as the most important revision the English Bible underwent before the final settlement of the Received Text. This was the work of some of those Protestant exiles who fled from the fires of persecution in their own land to the friendly shelter of the Reformed Churches abroad. They were scattered in various cities, in Frankfort, Strasburg, Basle, Zurich and Geneva. It is with those who settled in Geneva we are now concerned. John Knox the Scottish reformer was there; Miles Coverdale; Thomas Cole, once Dean of Salisbury; Christopher Goodman, formerly Divinity Professor at Oxford ; John Pullain, a translator of Ecclesiastes, Esther and other books of Scripture into English verse; Anthony Gilby, Thomas Sampson and William Whittingham. Sampson had been Dean of Chichester in Edward's time and afterwards became Dean of Christ Church in Elizabeth's reign, and Whittingham was afterwards Dean of Durham.

William Whittingham was the first among these exiles to take action in the matter of Bible translation. Born at Chester in 1524, at 16 he entered Brasenose College, graduating B.A. in 1540 and M.A. in 1547–8, having been elected Fellow of All Souls in 1545. In 1550 he went abroad for three years, spending his time chiefly at the University of Orleans, afterwards visiting the Universities of Germany and Geneva in 1552 and returning to England in 1553. Then came the time of exile when he went first to Frankfort and afterwards to Geneva, where he succeeded Knox as minister of the English congregation there. In 1557 he published, anonymously, a revised translation of the English New Testament. It is thus described : "The Newe Testament of Our Lord Jesus Christ. Conferred diligently with the Greke, and best approved translations. With the arguments as wel before the chapters, as for every Boke. At Geneva : Printed by Conrad Badius. MDLVII." The text of this version is based upon Tyndale's, compared with the Great Bible, and influenced by Beza's Latin translation. It formed the ground-work of the New Testament printed in the complete Genevan Bible of 1560, but is distinct from it. It was the first Testament to be printed in Roman type and also the first

23 Then the man faid, ‧ This now is bone of my bones, and flesh of my flesh: She shalbe called ‧ woman, becaufe she was taken out of man.

24 ‧ Therefore shal man leaue ‧ his father and his mother, and shal cleaue to his wife, and they shalbe one flesh.

25 And they were bothe naked, the man & his wife, and were not ‧ ashamed.

THE SITVACION OF THE GARDEN OF EDEN.

EVPHRATES
LA GRAND ARMENIE
TIGRIS AIS RIE
MESOPOTAMIE
BABYLON TERREDE HAVILA
BABYLONE
CHVS
LA CHEVTE DEVPHRATES ACHEVTE DE TIGRIS
LE GOLFE DE LA MER PERSIQVE.

La grand Armenie. Or, Armenia the great.

Terre de Hauilah. Or, Lãd of Hauilah.

La cheute d'Euphrates. Or, the fall of Euphrates.

La cheute de Tigris. Or, the fall of Tigris.

Le golfe de la mer Perfique. Or, the gulfe of the Perfian fea.

Becaufe mention is made in the tenth verfe of this feconde chapter of the riuer that watered the garden, we muste note that Euphrates and Tygris called in Ebrewe, Perash and Hiddekel, were called but one riuer where they ioyned together, als they had foure heades: that is, two as their fprings, & two where they fel into the Perfian fea. In this country and most plentiful land Adam dwelt, and this was called Paradise: that is, a garden of pleafure, becaufe of the frutefulnes and abundance thereof. And whereas it is faid that Tifhon compaffeth the land of Hauilah, it is meant of Tygris, which in fome place, as it paffed by diuers places, was called by fundry names, as fome time Diglito, in other places Pafitygris, & et fome Thefin or Tifhon. Likewife Euphrates towarde the countrey of Cush or Ethiopia, or Arabia was called Gihon. So that Tygris and Euphrates (which were but two riuers, and fome time when they ioyned together, were called after one name) were according to diuers places called by thefe foure names, fo that they might feme to haue bene foure diuers riuers.

CHAP. III.

2 *The woman feduced by the ferpent,* 6 *Entiseth her housband to finne.* 16 *They thre are punished.* 15 *Chrift is promifed.* 19 *Man is dust.* 23 *Man is cast out of paradise.*

NOw the ferpent was more ‧ fubtil then anie beaft of the field, which ‧ Lord God had made: and he ‧ faid to the woman, Yea, hathe God in dede faid, Ye shal not eat of euerie tre of the garden?

2 And the woman faid vnto the ferpent, We eat of the frute of the trees of the garden,

3 But of the frute of the tre, which is in the middes of the garden, God hathe faid, Ye shal not eat of it, nether shal ye touche it, ‧ lest ye dye.

4 Then *the ferpent faid to the woman, Ye shal not ‧ dye at all,

5 But God doeth knowe, that when ye shal eat thereof, your eyes shalbe opened, & ye shalbe as gods, ‧ knowing good and euil.

6 So the woman (feing that the tre was good for meat, and that it was pleafant to the eyes, & a tre to be defired to get knowledge) toke of the frute thereof, and did ‧ eat, and gaue alfo to her houfband with her, and he ‧ did eat.

7 Then the eyes of them bothe were opened, & they ‧ knewe that they were naked, and they fewed figtre leaues together, and made them felues ‧‧breeches.

8 ¶ Afterwarde they heard the voyce of

English version to adopt the division into verses made by Robert Estienne, the French printer, in his Greek Testament published at Geneva in 1551. With its elaborate apparatus it forms the first critical edition of the New Testament in English. The title-page of this work contains a curious woodcut representing Time raising Truth out of her grave, with this motto appended—"God by Tyme restoreth Truth, and maketh her victorious." There is an address to the reader giving some account of the work, and stating that the text has been "diligently revised by the most approved Greek examples and conference of translations in other tongues"; and for the profit of the reader the text has been "divided into verses and sections, according to the best editions in other languages."

It was not till three years later that this Genevan Testament of Whittingham's was followed by the complete Genevan Bible of 1560. The latter, unlike the former, was the joint production of several scholarly men, acting together for the attainment of one common end. In their preface they speak of the eminently favourable conditions under which they were able to work. And when we recall the circumstances of the time we can feel the force of what they say. As translators they were fortunate in the place where their work was done. For Geneva under the influence of Calvin had become the centre to

which were gathered some of the most eminent
Biblical scholars of the time.   And apart from their
fellow-countrymen, exiles like themselves, there was
at that time in Geneva a group of scholars who
were engaged in the work of correcting the French
version of Olivetan ; they therefore found themselves
in the company of men who though working in another
language were engaged in a task similar to their
own.   Then again they had the advantage of some
new Latin versions not accessible to previous translators.   Leo Juda had laboured for many years at
a new Latin version of the Old Testament, which
though left unfinished at his death was completed
by others ; and the Latin New Testament of Erasmus
having been revised by R. Gualther, the whole Bible
thus finished, was printed in 1544.   These Latin
versions and especially Beza's New Testament furnished important help to the English scholars in
what they regarded as their sacred task, and they
of course inherited also the result of the labours of
the English translators at home who had preceded
them.   In preparing the historical books they kept
in the main to the old renderings, merely altering
awkward or antiquated phrases here and there.
In the other parts of the work the changes were
more numerous.   Taking a passage from the 19th
chapter of Job Dr Westcott points out that there
is considerable originality in the version they gave.

Throughout the verses mentioned—"I am sure that my Redeemer liveth," &c.—he finds the French rendering widely different; of the ten changes introduced into the text of the Great Bible three of considerable importance are apparently original (7, 8, 10); and of the remainder one perhaps comes from Leo Juda (2), three from Pagninus (1, 5, 6), and two from Münster (4, 9). The Prophetical Books are revised after the manner adopted in the Historical Books, but with more numerous changes; the influence of the French translation being most marked in the Apocryphal Books. In all parts they appear to have taken the Great Bible as their basis, correcting its text without substituting for it a new translation. Dr Westcott concludes his examination of the Genevan Old Testament by saying—"there is abundant evidence to shew that they were perfectly competent to deal independently with points of Hebrew scholarship; and minute changes in expression shew that they were not indifferent to style."

This Genevan Bible, completed three years after the publication of the Genevan Testament, went forth to the world under the title: "The Bible and Holy Scriptures Conteyned in the Olde and Newe Testament. Translated According to the Ebrue and Greke, and conferred with the best translations in divers langages. With Moste Profitable Annotations...At Geneva. Printed by Ronland Hall.

M.D.LX. 4to." Below these words there is a wood-cut representing the Israelites crossing the Red Sea, and on the reverse of the title is a list of the books of the Bible, including the Apocrypha. Then follows a Dedication "to the moste vertuous and noble Quene Elizabeth" from her "humble subjects of the English Churche at Geneva"; and after this an Address "to our Beloved in the Lord, the Brethren of England, Scotland, Ireland etc.," dated "from Geneva, 10 April, 1560." In this Address, after pointing out that the former translations required greatly to be reformed, the translators went on to say, "Not that we vindicate anything to ourselves above the rest of our brethren (for God knoweth with what fear and trembling we have been for the space of two years and more, day and night, occupied herein), but being earnestly desired, and by divers, whose learning and godliness we reverence, exhorted...we undertook this great and wonderful work (with all reverence, as in the presence of God, as entreating the Word of God, whereunto we think ourselves insufficient), which now God, according to his Divine providence and mercy hath directed to a most prosperous end...God is our witness that we have by all means endeavoured to set forth the purity of the Word and right sense of the Holy Ghost, for the edifying of the brethren in faith and charity."

Contrary to what we should have expected the Testament included in the complete Bible of 1560 differs from the Testament of 1557 in nearly forty places. In thirty-three of these the rendering is new, and in sixteen the alteration still maintains its ground. Recognising these facts Dr W. F. Moulton concluded that the Testament is a careful revision of Tyndale, and that the Bible is again a careful revision of the Testament; on the whole, too, Beza's influence tended greatly to the improvement of the work, for by this mistakes were removed which had disfigured all preceding versions. Very many of the changes in the English-Genevan New Testament have passed from that into our own Bible. Archbishop Trench in his work on the Authorised Version quoted five passages to show "the very good and careful scholarship brought to bear upon the Genevan revision," in which "it is the first to seize the exact meaning...which all the preceding versions had missed." These are all derived from Beza. One other point should be noticed to which Professor Plumptre called attention—the Genevan version (in both forms) "omits the name of St Paul from the title to the Epistle to the Hebrews, and, in a short preface, leaves the authorship an open question." The explanatory notes in this version were prepared by the Genevan translators, and with considerable care. In the Epistle to the Romans, for example,

there are about 220 of these, and many also elsewhere, forming a kind of condensed commentary,
supplying historical and geographical information
and clearing up obscure texts, but more often
giving pithy observations on the narrative, as when
we are told that "Lot, thinking to get paradise
found a hell." We can well believe what we have
been told that its phrases found echo in Scripture
quotation from Shakespeare to Bunyan.

The expense connected with the production of
this version of 1560, which must have been considerable, was defrayed by the English community in
Geneva, "whose hearts," as the translators themselves
tell us, "God touched to encourage the revisers not
to spare any charges for the furtherance of such a
benefit and favour of God." Among the contributors
was John Bodley the father of the founder of the
great Bodleian Library. Possibly for prominent
service in this way rendered he received from Queen
Elizabeth a patent dated January 8, 1561, securing to
him for seven years the exclusive right to print in
England the version which first came out in Geneva.
The second edition of this version, the first in folio,
published in 1562, appears to have been sent forth by
him though no printer's name is attached to the
work.

As already stated the complete Genevan Bible,
unlike the Genevan Testament of William Whitting-

ham by which it was preceded, was the joint production of several workers. Lelong says that the chief of those employed upon it were Coverdale, Whittingham and Gilby, but he mentions also Goodman, Sampson, Cole, "and certain others" as sharing in it. The completion of the work, however, seems to have fallen finally into the hands of Whittingham, Gilby and Sampson alone. Anthony à Wood gives the same six names as those mentioned by Lelong, but goes on to say that "before the greater part was finished, Queen Mary died. So that the Protestant religion appearing again in England, the exiled divines left Frankfort and Geneva, and returned into England. Howbeit, Whittingham with one or two more, being resolved to go through with the work, did tarry at Geneva a year and a half after Queen Elizabeth came to the Crown."

The work thus produced by Englishmen in exile found truest welcome among Englishmen at home. For nearly a hundred years the Genevan Bible was the favourite version of the common people. Several reasons would account for this. For one thing, being in quarto shape, it was more easy to handle than the big folios which went before it. It was also easier to read, the type being in Roman and Italic, not Gothic; and easier for reference, retaining as it did the divisions into chapters and verses made by Estienne for the New Testament and by others for the Old

B.   6

Testament. It retained also the marginal notes of 1557; indicated by accentual marks the pronunciation of proper names; and in addition had woodcuts and convenient maps and tables. But most of all, next to the Bible itself, its notes and comments made it a welcome book to the devout men and women of Puritan days. Between its publication in 1560 and the appearance of the Authorised Version of 1611 it went through sixty editions; and even after the Authorised Version had appeared, ten more editions were added to the sixty which went before. Right on to the days of the Civil War it continued to be the Bible of the Puritan household.

In 1576 a revised edition of the book was brought out by Laurence Tomson, private secretary to Sir Francis Walsingham, which while leaving the Old Testament unchanged, made alterations in the New. He entitled it "The New Testament, translated from the Greek by Theodore Beza." It was dedicated to F. Walsingham and F. Hastings and became so popular that it was frequently substituted for the Genevan Testament in the Genevan Bible. The text is not much altered but the commentary in the margin received enlargement. One of the peculiarities of this version is that Tomson closely followed Beza, putting "that" or "this" for the *ille* by which Beza had rendered the emphatic force of the Greek article, as for example in John i. 1 "In the beginning was *that* Word." The grotesque effect of this is seen in Tomson's rendering of 1 John v. 12 "He that hath *that* Son hath *that* life : and he that hath not *that* Son of God hath not *that* life." With his commentary he seems to have been himself well pleased, for he says of it, " I dare avouch it, and whoso readeth it shall so find it, that there is not one hard sentence nor dark speech nor doubtful word, but is so opened and hath such light given to it, that children may go through with it, and the simplest that are may walk without any guide, without wandering and going astray."

In 1576, the same year this revision by Tomson appeared, there appeared also the first English Bible printed in Scotland. It is the Genevan version, the title expressed in the same words, with the difference that it is stated to be "Printed In Edinbrugh Be Alexander Arbuthnet, Printer to the Kingis Maiestie, dwelling at yᵉ Kirk of feild. 1579." The title of the New Testament portion is in this form : "At Edinburgh, Printed by Thomas Bassandyne M.D.LXXVI Fol." It is an exact reprint of the first folio edition of 1561–2. Bassandyne's name does not appear on the title of the Old Testament, which was the last to be printed, being completed by his colleague Alexander Arbuthnet in 1579, Bassandyne dying in the interval. By order of the General Assembly every parish in Scotland subscribed a fixed amount before the work was undertaken, the price being £4. 13*s*. 4*d*. Scots currency. So firm was the hold this book gained in the country that as late as the close of the 18th century a Genevan Bible was still in use in the church of Crail in Fifeshire.

Though in the earlier years of Elizabeth's reign four editions of Tyndale's Testament are assigned to the years 1561, 1566, 1570, it does not appear that the Bibles of Coverdale, Taverner or Matthew were ever reprinted after 1553. The only two versions, therefore, which were publicly prominent were the Great Bible and the Genevan version. And as between these two, the superiority of the text and translation of the latter and its increasing popularity made it very unlikely that it would ever be superseded by the former. Yet the Genevan Bible could never with the Bishops' consent become the only Bible of the nation. Not because it was Calvinistic in doctrine in its notes and commentary, for the bishops them-selves were Calvinistic in those days, but because in its general trend it was hostile to the episcopal church system. Not only did it again and again translate the word " ecclesia " not by " church," but by " congregation "; but in its exposition of the meaning of " locusts " in Revelation ix. 3, for example, we come upon such a passage as this: " Locusts are false teachers, heretics, and worldly subtle prelates, with monks, friars, cardinals, patriarchs, archbishops, bishops, doctors, bachelors and masters, which forsake Christ to maintain false doctrine." Clearly this kind of teaching must not be permitted to go forth tacked on to the Bible and unchallenged. Archbishop Parker, therefore, who had been consecrated in 1559, took the matter in hand somewhere about 1563–4. Strype tells us that he "took upon him the labour to contrive and set the whole work agoing in a proper method by sorting out the whole Bible into parcels... and distributing those parcels to able bishops and learned men, to peruse and collate each the book or books allotted them : sending withal his instructions for the method they should observe." In a letter preserved under date 1566 among the State Papers, though probably belonging to an earlier year, Parker writes to Sir William Cecil, telling him how he has "distributed the Bible in parts to divers men," and even going so far in courtliness to that great statesman as to express the hope that he will undertake the revision of some "one epistle of St Paul, or Peter or James."

Another letter from Parker to Cecil gives the facts concerning the separate distribution of the work. He himself, in addition to prefaces and other introductory matter, undertook to translate Genesis and Exodus in the Old Testament, and Matthew and Mark, then from 2 Corinthians to Hebrews inclusive, in the New Testament. Richard Davies, the Bishop of St David's, a man who had laboured zealously for the spiritual good of his native country of Wales, took the translation from Joshua to 2 Kings, that is, 2 Samuel, while Sandys, Bishop of Worcester, continued the work on to the end of Chronicles. William Alley, who had succeeded Coverdale as Bishop of Exeter, translated Deuteronomy. Miles Coverdale, though still living after his resignation of his See, took no part in the work, he being now an old man over eighty. Parkhurst, Bishop of Norwich, along with Barlow, Bishop of Chichester, made himself responsible for the Apocryphal books ; Andrew Perne, Master of Peterhouse and Dean of Ely, translated Ecclesiastes and Canticles. The Bishop of Winchester was the translator from Isaiah to Lamentations, and the Bishop of Lichfield and Coventry of the rest of the Greater Prophets, while Grindal, Bishop of London, took the Minor Prophets. Coming again to the New Testament, the Bishop of Peterborough translated the Gospels according to Luke and John, the Bishop of Ely the Acts and the Romans, the Dean of Westminster the 1st Epistle to the Corinthians, and the Bishop of Lincoln the General Epistles to the book of Revelation. Altogether there were eight of the bishops concerned in the undertaking, a fact which gave the name to the book of "The Bishops' Bible." It was published in folio in 1568, the colophon intimating that it was "Imprinted at London in povvles Churchyarde by Richard Jugge." A splended copy was presented to the Queen, the accompanying letter

THE BISHOPS' BIBLE: 1568

From Mr W. Aldis Wright's copy

bearing date October 5, 1568. The Bible itself has no dedication, but in the centre of the title is a portrait of the Queen; and at the beginning of Joshua and the Psalter portraits of the Earl of Leicester and Cecil are introduced. It was furnished also with a table of the books of the Old Testament with tables of lessons and psalms, an almanac and calendar, two prologues, a chronological table and table of contents; woodcuts, maps and other tables were also introduced.

When the book was ready for publication, the Archbishop through Cecil endeavoured to obtain the Queen's recognition on its behalf, with what result does not appear. Eventually Convocation in the "Constitutions and Canons Ecclesiastical," of April 1571, ordered that every archbishop and bishop should have at his house a copy of the Holy Bible of the largest volume, as lately printed at London; and that it should be placed in the hall or large dining-room, that it might be useful to their servants or strangers. Each cathedral also should have a copy, and "as far as it could be conveniently done," all the churches. Later on, in the Articles issued by Archbishop Whitgift in 1583, the 10th ordered "that one kind of translation of the Bible be only used in public service, as well in churches as chapels, and that to be the same which is now authorized by the consent of the bishops." The adoption of the Bible thus authorized, if not by the Crown, by Canons Ecclesiastical, and by the Archbishop, does not seem to have been readily or universally made. One reason may have been its costliness. The price at which the first edition was sold in 1571 was 27*s*. 8*d*. or about £16 in present value. Still a second edition, in a small quarto volume, was issued in 1569, a third of the Bible, and an edition of the New Testament only, followed in 1570, 1571. In all about forty editions of this version appear to have been published, one half of these containing the whole Bible. It seems certain that while the Genevan held its own the Great Bible was entirely displaced by the Bishops'; no edition of it appearing to be printed after 1569. It is however not to be forgotten that the Book of Psalms in the new revision had to yield in the end to that in the Great Bible. The edition of 1572 prints both in parallel columns—one properly belonging to the version, the other taken from the Great Bible.

That there were defects in this version we might expect from the way in which it was brought about. The work was, as we have seen, given out in parcels to different men; each man acted independently, and there was no common meeting for the purpose of discussing the various renderings. The final revision was left in the hands of Parker himself, who, as Archbishop, was a very busy man, and not conspicuously eminent as a scholar; and one at least of the others did not give very much time to his task. It is said that the revision of the books of Kings and Chronicles was despatched in about seven weeks by Bishop Sandys. As to the comparative value of the version as a whole we are fortunate in possessing the deliberate judgment of two eminent members of the Revision Company who brought out the Revised Version of 1881—Bishop Westcott and Dr W. F. Moulton. They are agreed in the opinion that the Greek scholarship of the revisers of the Bishops' Bible is superior to their Hebrew scholarship. Dr Westcott says that in the Historical Books of the Old Testament they followed the text of the Great Bible very closely. They were lacking in independence: "The influence of the Genevan revision is perceptible throughout, but it is more obvious in the Prophets than elsewhere." He concludes by saying, "There is but little to recommend the original renderings of the Bishops' Bible in the Old Testament. As a general rule they appear to be arbitrary and at variance with the exact sense of the Hebrew text." In like manner Dr Moulton, after examining the passage in 2 Samuel xxiii. 1—7, where in seven verses the Great Bible and the Bishops' differ about 18 times, finds that 15 of the new renderings in the latter are taken from the Genevan version. Of the 18 changes 13 may be called improvements; with one exception they are derived from the Genevan

Bible, from which also come two changes which are clearly for the worse. About 12 better renderings found in the Genevan Bible are at the same time here neglected. After examining one or two other passages Dr Moulton gives judgment by saying: "The conclusion from this investigation is not very favourable to the Bishops' Bible. In the Old Testament Cranmer's Bible was too closely followed and improvements which were ready to the hand of the translators were not appreciated. What is original in this version does not often possess any great merit."

So far as the New Testament is concerned, the second edition was carefully revised. Dr Westcott takes the passage in Ephesians iv. 7—16 as an illustration of how much merit is due to this part of the work. Having shown that in this passage the Great Bible and the Bishops' differ in 26 places, he adds: "Of these 26 variations no less than 16 are new, while only 10 are due to the Genevan version, and the character of the original corrections marks a very close and thoughtful revision, based faithfully upon the Greek." He further shows that throughout the entire epistle the changes amount to nearly 50, and among the new readings are some phrases which have become very familiar to us, as "*less than the least of all saints*"; "*middle wall* of partition"; "*fellow-citizens* with the saints."

It may be mentioned that copies of the chief editions of the Bishops' Bible are preserved in the British Museum, in the Universities of Oxford and Cambridge, in the Rylands' Library, and in that of the British and Foreign Bible Society.

And now at this point a notable fact occurred. As the Genevan version of 1560 was followed in the way of correction by the Bishops' Bible of 1568, so this again was followed with the same purpose by the Roman Catholic version of the New Testament in English, known as the *Rheims-Douai Bible* of 1582. It was printed abroad and appeared in England bearing the following elaborate title: "The New Testament of Jesus Christ, Translated Faithfully into English, out of the authentical Latin, according to the best corrected copies of the same, diligently conferred with the Greeke and other editions in divers languages: With Arguments of bookes and chapters, Annotations and other necessarie helps, for the better understanding of the text, and specially for the discoverie of the Corruptions of divers late translations, and for cleering the Controversies in religion in these daies; in the English College of Rhemes. Ps. 118, 'Give me understanding, and I will search Thy law.' Those things specially must be commended to memorie which make most against Heretikes: whose deceites cease not to circumvent and beguile al the weaker sort and the more negligent persons. Printed at

Rhemes, by John Fogny. 1582. Cum privilegio."
This version was the work of Roman Catholics who
had fled from persecution in Elizabeth's time and
were connected with the Seminary at Douai and the
English College at Rheims.   The translation was
made from the Latin Vulgate by three men—Gregory
Martin, William (afterwards Cardinal) Allen and
Richard Bristow.   The first-named was the one most
actively concerned in the work.   He had been a
scholar of St John's, Oxford; in 1570, the year of
Elizabeth's excommunication, he went over to Douai
and then became divinity reader at Rheims.   Wood
speaks of him as "an excellent linguist, exactly read
and versed in the Sacred Scriptures and went beyond
all of his time in humane literature."   He was also the
writer of an appendix to the Testament entitled "A
Discovery of the Manifold Corruptions of the Holy
Scriptures by the Heretics of our Days," in which he
endeavoured to overturn all Protestant versions and
so clear the ground for the new version now being
sent forth.   He was answered by Dr Fulke, Master
of Pembroke Hall, Cambridge, who published a
"Defence of the sincere and true translation of the
Holy Scriptures into the English tongue, against the
manifold cavils of Gregory Martin."   In the preface in
which the translators of the Rheims version state their
object they frankly say that it is not their idea that
the Scriptures should always be printed in the mother

tongue and be freely read by all. That was not the belief of their Church, as was testified by the Constitutions of Arundel and by that decree of the Council of Trent which said that the Scriptures "may not be indifferently read of all men, nor of any other than of such as have express licence thereunto of their lawful ordinaries." Their forefathers did not suffer every sciolist to translate, or every husbandman, artificer, prentice, maid and man to read the Bible, making it the subject of table-talk for "ale-benches, boats and barges." They repudiate the idea that it is from envy that the priests keep the holy book from the people. The reason is that the Church would have "the unworthy repelled, the curious repressed, the simple measured, the learned humbled, and all sorts so to use them, or to abstain from them, as is most convenient for every one's salvation." Their sole purpose now in sending forth the Bible in the vernacular is "for the more speedy abolishing of a number of false and impious translations put forth by sundry sectes, and for the better preservation or reclaime of many good soules endangered thereby."

In choosing the text of Scripture from which to translate they also frankly admit that they have not selected the original Greek, but the Latin Vulgate translation of the Greek. They have done so because the latter was in use in the Church 1300 years ago ; it is that which St Jerome corrected according to the

Greek by appointment of Damasus the Pope; it was commended by Augustine; has been used in the Church's service; has been declared of the Council of Trent of all Latin translations to be only authentical; and it is the gravest, sincerest, of greatest majesty, least partiality, as being without all respect of controversies and contentions, especially those of our time. After giving other reasons they conclude with one which should have rendered all others unnecessary when they say that the Vulgate "is not only better than all other Latin translations but than the Greek text itself in those places where they disagree." For the first heretics were Greeks and the Greek Scriptures suffered much at their hands. The Hebrew text was said to have been foully corrupted by the Jews, and the Greek by heretics. This apology in effect admits that the Rheims version has no independent authority as a text. Still it is to be remembered on the other side that Jerome's Latin translation was derived from Greek MSS. more ancient than any we now possess, and is sometimes, therefore, of great value as giving us in disputed passages the text current in the earliest times, and its testimony is in some cases confirmed by MSS. discovered in more recent times. This merit is however minimized by the fact that the common copies of the Vulgate, of which the Douai Bible is one, have not always preserved the pure Latin text of Jerome, but have been deteriorated in the course of constant copying from one generation to another. The need of new examination was recognised even as early as the Council of Trent.

The Rhemish translators deserve credit for their treatment of the Greek article. As the Latin language has no definite article it might be supposed that this would be a weak point with them. But it is not so. Dr Moulton discovered, in a comparatively hasty search, more than forty instances in which, of all versions from Tyndale to the Authorised Version included, the Rhemish alone is correct in regard to the Article. Its translators had evidently made use of the Greek text as well as that of the Vulgate. They have also preserved significant phrases of the original and impressive arrangement of words such as "the liberty of the glory of the children of God"; "holiness of truth"; "by their fruits ye shall know them"; "ye are not come to a palpable mountain." Then, too, the translation "our lamps are going out" is unquestionably correct; and there are phrases in the 1st chapter of the Epistle of James, such as "upbraideth not"; "nothing wavering"; "the engrafted word"; and "bridleth not," which are effective as well as correct. It may be added to this that Dr Westcott has given a list of Latin words from a single Epistle which King James's translators have taken from the Rhemish Testament; *separated* (Rom. i. 1), *impenitent*(ii. 5), *approvest*(ii. 18), *propitiation* (iii. 25), *remission* (id.), *glory* in tribulations (v. 3), *commendeth* (v. 8), *concupiscence* (vii. 7), *expectation* (viii. 19), *confession is made* unto salvation (x. 10), *emulation* (xi. 14), *conformed* (xii. 2).

As we might expect, the trend of the translation in some places is unduly in the direction of Romish doctrine, as, for example, when we read : "In those dayes cometh John the Baptist preaching in the desert of Jewrie, saying, Doe penance." Similarly, "If you have not penance, you shall all likewise perish," and "Not willing that any perish, but that all return to penance"; "Remember your prelates which have spoken the word of God to you"; "By good works make your calling and election sure." But apart from this tendency there were renderings which to Englishmen must have been as an unknown tongue and could scarcely be called translations : for example, instead of "He humbled himself," we read "he exinanited himself"; "The passions of this time are not condigne to the glory to come"; "Our wrestling is against Princes and Potestas, against the rectors of the world of this darkness, against the spirituals of wickedness in the celestials"; "Give us today our supersubstantial bread." An English reader must have been in sheer despair, when, as a translation of Psalm lvii. 10, he read the following : "Before your thorns did understand the old briar : as living so in wrath he swalloweth them." With a similar feeling he must also have greeted such words as these: odible, coinquination, correption, exprobrate, longanimity, obsecration, and scenopegia. No wonder that Thomas Fuller called this book "a translation needing to be translated."

The Old Testament portion of this version was not published till 1609 and 1610 though it seems to have been ready at the same time as the New Testament in 1582. The delay arose from lack of means, or as they express it, from the "one general cause our poore estate in banishment." It appeared under the title: "The Holie Bible Faithfully Translated into English Out Of The Authentical Latin. Diligently conferred with the Hebrew, Greeke, and other editions in divers languages....By the English College Of Doway...Printed at Doway by Laurence Kellam, at the Signe of the bolie Lambe. M.DC.IX (-M.DC.X.) 2 vols. 4to." The complete work was reprinted in Rouen in 1635. In 1749–50, and again in 1763–4, editions of the Douai Old Testament and the Rheims New Testament were published, each edition in five volumes. This revised form is substantially the version used at the present day by English-speaking Roman Catholics.

B.

CHAPTER VI

THE AUTHORISED VERSION OF 1611

When James I came to the English throne in 1603, after the appearance of the Bishops' Bible in 1568, there had been no further revision of the Scriptures for more than a generation. The Great Bible of 1539, partly because it was heavy and costly, and partly also because it had been superseded by the Bishops' Bible, had long ceased to be reprinted. Old copies, no doubt, were still to be found here and there in village churches, but there were no new issues. And yet that Bible by which it had been superseded had not really taken firm and enduring hold of the popular mind. Dean Plumptre said, and said truly, that "of all the English versions the Bishops' Bible had probably the least success. It did not command the respect of scholars, and its size and cost were far from meeting the wants of the people. Its circulation appears to have been practically limited to the churches which were ordered to be supplied with it." There were only six editions in quarto and one in octavo; the other thirteen were in folio. On the other hand, the Genevan version retained its unrivalled popularity. Between 1568 and 1611 there were no fewer than sixteen editions in octavo, fifty-two in quarto and eighteen in folio. Thus there seemed to be little prospect of unity in the matter of Bible usage. For the Genevan version was too pronouncedly puritan in its notes and comments to be acceptable to the authorities of the Church; while the version favoured by the bishops had too many drawbacks ever to win its way among the people at large. So matters remained till the beginning of the reign of King James I, when, as one may say, in an almost accidental way, a new version was projected and prepared—that of the Authorised Version of 1611, which ultimately had the happy effect of uniting the whole nation for more than two centuries and a half in the use of the same book as the household Bible of the English people.

James I was proclaimed King on the 24th of March 1603, and on the 7th of the following May he entered London to take possession of the throne. Between these two dates, and while he was the guest of the Cromwells of Hinchinbrook, near Huntingdon, he was approached by certain of the puritan clergy who presented him with what is known as the Millenary Petition. This was a petition for the

7—2

abolition of certain usages in the Church which they regarded as superstitious and savouring of Rome ; also against "longsomeness of service, profanation of the Lord's Day, and against excommunication by such lay persons as the archdeacon's commissary, and without the consent of pastors." They had "some good conference with his Majesty and gave him a book of reasons." Though no definite answer was given to their plea at the time, it was not altogether fruitless ; for the following October the King appointed a meeting to be held in January, 1604, for the hearing and determining "things pretended to be amiss in the Church." This meeting has taken its place in history as the Hampton Court Conference, and it is said that on the second day of this Conference, Dr Reynolds, the leader of the Puritans, "moved his Majesty that there might be a new translation of the Bible, because those which were allowed in the reign of King Henry VIII and Edward VI were corrupt and not answerable to the truth of the original." Though this statement is made in Dr Barlow's "Sum and Substance of the Conference at Hampton Court," there is reason to doubt whether it gives a quite accurate account of what actually took place. The Puritans were somewhat roughly handled at that Conference, and were there only to plead for concessions to their views which they knew the bishops were unwilling to grant,

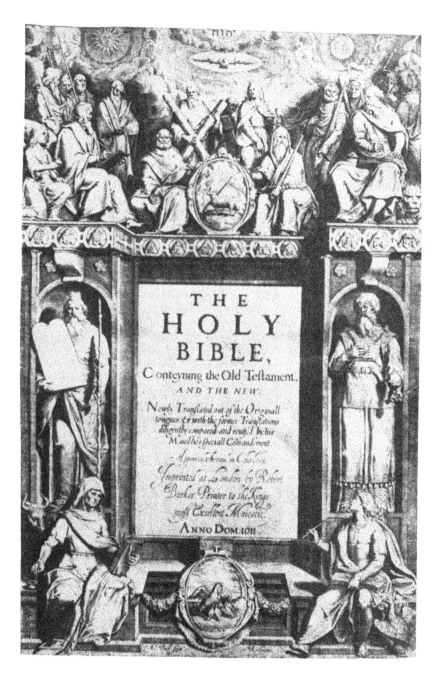

TITLE PAGE OF THE AUTHORISED VERSION: 1611

From a copy in the Library of Emmanuel College, Cambridge

and that they should, under such circumstances, have been the originators of the idea of a new Authorised Version seems somewhat improbable. Moreover, it is at variance with what the translators of that version have themselves told us in that preface of theirs prefixed to the version. What is there said is as follows :—" The very historical truth is, the Conference having been appointed for hearing the complaints of the Puritans, and when by force of reason they were put from all other grounds, they had recourse at the last to this shift, that they could not with good conscience subscribe to the Communion Book [the Book of Common Prayer] since it maintained the Bible as it was there translated, which was, as they said, a most corrupted translation. And although this was judged to be but a very poor and empty shift, yet even hereupon did his Majesty begin to bethink himself of the good that might ensue by a new translation, and presently after gave order for this translation which is now presented." This is a much more probable account, it is the account given by the translators themselves, and from it we are entitled to say that the idea of the Authorised Version of King James was really started by King James himself. It is clear the King was more in earnest about the matter then than any one else. Some of the bishops, at any rate, looked coldly upon it. Bancroft, Bishop of London, said at the time that "if every man's humour was to be followed, there would be no end of translating." The King thought otherwise, thought that pains ought to be taken to secure one uniform translation, to be made by the best learned in both the Universities, reviewed by the bishops, then presented to the Privy Council and finally ratified by his royal authority : "and so this whole Church to be bound unto it and none other." Thus in this unexpected, and almost accidental way, came about the first conception of that Authorised Version whose Tercentenary we are now celebrating in 1911.

In the practical carrying out of that conception, again, the King was most actively concerned. Convocation met shortly after the Conference, but not a word appears to have been said there on the proposed revision. The King, however, did not let the matter fall into forgetfulness. He must have been already making enquiries at the Universities as to what learned men there were fit for the enterprise, for on the 22nd of July, 1604, he wrote to the Bishop of London telling him that he had chosen fifty-four translators to meet in various companies at Westminster, Oxford and Cambridge, under the presidency of the Hebrew professors of the two Universities and the Dean of Westminster. He further asked him to move the bishops to inform themselves of all such learned men within their several dioceses as had especial skill in the Hebrew and Greek tongues, and to write to them urging them to send any observations they had made on previous translations to Mr Lively the Hebrew reader in Cambridge, or to Dr Harding the Hebrew reader in Oxford, or to Dr Andrewes, Dean of Westminster, to be by them imparted to their several companies.

It is somewhat surprising to find that the scheme so promptly outlined hung fire for the next three years, nothing further being done, so far as we know, till 1607. From that point, however, the work proceeded with vigour. The fifty-four learned men mentioned by the King, but afterwards, possibly by death, reduced to forty-seven, were divided into six companies, four for the Old Testament and Apocrypha and two for the New Testament. The company meeting at Westminster under the presidency of the Dean, the saintly Lancelot Andrewes, and consisting of ten persons, were to undertake the revision of Genesis on to 2 Kings inclusive. The company meeting at Cambridge, and consisting of eight persons, were to take from 1 Chronicles to Ecclesiastes inclusive. The company meeting at Oxford, consisting of seven persons, were to make themselves responsible for the Prophets from Isaiah to Malachi. A separate company, also meeting at Cambridge, were to undertake the Apocrypha. Then, as to the New Testament, a second company meeting at Oxford were charged with the revision of the Four Gospels, the Acts and the Apocalypse, a second Westminster company taking from Romans to Jude inclusive.

Rules for the guidance of these different companies were elaborately drawn up beforehand. They were to take the Bishops' Bible as their basis, altering it as little as the truth of the original would permit; the names of prophets and writers and also other names in the text were to be given as commonly used, and the old ecclesiastical words to be kept, as, for example, the word *church* was not to be translated *congregation*. The translations by Tyndale, Matthews, Coverdale, and those of the Great Bible and the Genevan Version were to be used when agreeing better with the text than the Bishops' Bible. Each separate translator was first to go over the part assigned to him by himself alone, then all were to meet together, confer as to what they had done, and agree as to what should stand. Selden in his *Table Talk* tells us further as to their method of procedure. They took, says he, an excellent way : " That part of the Bible was given to him who was most excellent in such a tongue, and then they met together and one read the translation, the rest holding in their hands some Bible, either of the learned tongues, or French, Spanish, Italian, &c. : if they found any fault, they spoke ; if not, he read on."

When the several companies had completed the portions assigned to them, there would still be a necessity for general supervision. So far as we know the six companies never met as one body, but when three years had been spent in revision, the writer of the life of John Bois tells us, arrangements were made for a general supervision : "The whole work being finished, and three copies of the whole Bible sent from Cambridge, Oxford and Westminster to London, a new choice was to be made of six in all, two out of every company, to review the whole work, and extract one copy out of all these to be committed to the press, for the dispatch of which business Mr Downes and Mr Bois were sent for up to London, where meeting their fellow-labourers, they went daily to Stationers' Hall, and in three-quarters of a year fulfilled their task, all which time they had from the Company of Stationers thirty shillings each per week duly paid them. Last of all Bilson, Bishop of Winchester, and Dr Miles Smith, again reviewed the whole work, and prefixed arguments to the several books."

The three years of slow and patient scholarship spent on the Authorised Version were not completed without a certain touch of pathos. It has often been told how the Venerable Bede completed the translation of John's Gospel in the closing hours of life. "It is completed now," said the boy scribe. "Thou hast said the truth," replied the dying man, "all is ended. Take my head in thy hands. I would sit in the holy place in which I was wont to pray." And seated there, while he chanted the *Gloria*, his soul passed away. A kindred story has come down to us concerning Dr Reynolds, one of the translators of the version of 1611, of whom Thomas Fuller says you could never tell which was greater, his learning or his goodness. He was one of the company engaged upon the Books of the Prophets, but in the course of the work he was seized with consumption, and slowly faded out of life. Yet as Featley tells us, "for his great skill in the Originall Languages," the other members of the company had recourse to him "once a weeke and in his Lodgings perfected their Notes." In a great part of the sickness of which he died the meeting was held in his rooms at Corpus Christi, in Oxford, "and he, lying on his Pallet, assisted them, and in a manner, in the very translation of the booke of life, was translated to a better life."

The striking document which all the revisers adopted as their preface to the New Version was drawn up by Dr Miles Smith, afterwards Bishop of Gloucester. As serious-minded men they felt, they said, the importance of the work they had taken in hand. There was need of translation, for translation it is that openeth the window to let in the light; that breaketh the shell that we may eat the kernel;

ſaying, This man receiueth ſinners, and eateth with them.

3 ¶ And he ſpake this parable vnto them, ſaying,

Math.18 11.

4 What man of you hauing an hundred ſheepe, if he looſe one of them, doeth not leaue the ninety and nine in the wilderneſſe, and goe after that which is loſt, vntill he finde it?

5 And when he hath found it, hee layeth it on his ſhoulders, reioycing.

6 And when he commeth home, he calleth together his friends, and neighbours, ſaying vnto them, Reioyce with me, for I haue found my ſheepe which was loſt.

7 I ſay vnto you, that likewiſe ioy ſhall bee in heauen ouer one ſinner that repenteth, more then ouer ninety and nine iuſt perſons, which need no repentance.

8 ¶ Either what woman hauing ten pieces of ſiluer, if ſhe loſe one piece, doeth not light a candle, and ſweepe the houſe, and ſeeke diligently till ſhe finde it?

[Drachma was a piece of ſiluer of the value of the eight part of an ounce. 15.d. halfe peny, which is more then our peny, Mark.12.41]

9 And when ſhe hath found it, ſhe calleth her friends and her neighbours together, ſaying, Reioyce with me, for I haue found the piece which I had loſt.

10 Likewiſe I ſay vnto you, there is ioy in the preſence of the Angels of God, ouer one ſinner that repenteth.

11 ¶ And hee ſaid, A certaine man had two ſonnes:

12 And the yonger of them ſaid to his father, Father, giue me the portion of goods that falleth to me. And he diuided vnto them his liuing.

13 And not many dayes after, the yonger ſonne gathered all together, and tooke his iourney into a farre countrey, and there waſted his ſubſtance with riotous liuing.

14 And when he had ſpent all, there aroſe a mighty famine in that land, and he began to be in want.

15 And he went and ioyned himſelfe to a citizen of that countrey, and he ſent him into his fields to feed ſwine.

16 And he would faine haue filled his belly with the huſkes that the ſwine did eate: and no man gaue vnto him.

17 And when hee came to himſelfe, hee ſaid, How many hired ſeruants of my fathers haue bread ynough and to ſpare, and I periſh with hunger?

18 I will ariſe and goe to my father, and will ſay vnto him, Father, I

haue ſinned againſt heauen and before thee.

19 And am no more worthy to bee called thy ſonne: make me as one of thy hired ſeruants.

20 And he aroſe and came to his father. But when hee was yet a great way off, his father ſaw him, and had compaſſion, and ranne, and fell on his necke, and kiſſed him.

21 And the ſonne ſaid vnto him, Father, I haue ſinned againſt heauen, and in thy ſight, and am no more worthy to be called thy ſonne.

22 But the father ſaid to his ſeruants, Bring foorth the beſt robe, and put it on him, and put a ring on his hand, and ſhooes on his feet.

23 And bring hither the fatted calfe, and kill it, and let vs eate and be merry.

24 For this my ſonne was dead, and is aliue againe; he was loſt, & is found. And they began to be merry.

25 Now his elder ſonne was in the field, and as he came and drew nigh to the houſe, he heard muſicke & dauncing.

26 And he called one of the ſeruants, and aſked what theſe things meant.

27 And he ſaid vnto him, Thy brother is come, and thy father hath killed the fatted calfe, becauſe he hath receiued him ſafe and ſound.

28 And he was angry, and would not goe in: therefore came his father out, and intreated him.

29 And he anſwering ſaid to his father, Loe, theſe many yeeres doe I ſerue thee, neither tranſgreſſed I at any time thy commandement, and yet thou neuer gaueſt me a kidde, that I might make merry with my friends:

30 But as ſoone as this thy ſonne was come, which hath deuoured thy liuing with harlots, thou haſt killed for him the fatted calfe.

31 And he ſaid vnto him, Sonne, thou art euer with mee, and all that I haue is thine.

32 It was meete that wee ſhould make merry, and bee glad: for this thy brother was dead, and is aliue againe: and was loſt, and is found.

CHAP. XVI.

1 The parable of the vniuſt ſteward. 14 Chriſt reprooueth the hypocriſie of the couetous Phariſees. 19 The rich glutton, and Lazarus the begger.

D2   And

that putteth aside the curtain that we may look into the most holy places. By doing the work they had done they had no thought of disparaging those who had been in the field before them. Rather they acknowledged them as having been raised up of God for the building and furnishing of His Church, and deserve to be had of posterity in everlasting remembrance. If they, building upon their foundation and being helped by their labours, are only trying to make that better which they left so good, no man would have cause to mislike them; indeed their predecessors, if they were alive, would thank them. When they took up the work at first it was no thought of theirs that they had to make a new translation, nor yet to make a bad one a good one, but to make a good one better, or, out of many good ones one principal good one, not justly to be excepted against. They felt they had to tread a difficult path, for it is hard to please all even when we please God best. For he that meddleth with men's religion in any part meddleth with their custom, nay, with their freehold. Yet, though difficult, how important the work! For what is piety without truth? What truth, what saving truth without the Word of God? What Word of God whereof we may be sure without the Scriptures? If we are ignorant they will instruct us; if out of the way they will bring us home; if in heaviness they will comfort us; if dull quicken us; if cold inflame us. The Bible is not only an armour but also a whole armoury of weapons both offensive and defensive ; it is not merely a tree but a whole paradise of trees of life.   It is a treasury of most costly jewels, a fountain of most pure water springing up unto everlasting life.   With wise thoughts like these, thus briefly summarised, the translators commend their readers to God and to the Spirit of His grace, which is able to build further than we can ask or think.

In 1611 the book upon which they had laboured so faithfully appeared from the press of Robert Barker, Printer to the King's Most Excellent Majesty. The title occupies the centre of an engraving, on the right and left of which are the figures of Moses and Aaron, with the Four Evangelists at the corners.   At the top in Hebrew characters is the sacred name of God, with the Holy Dove beneath.   The New Testament has a separate title within a woodcut border representing along one side the badges of the twelve tribes of Israel, and along the other the twelve Apostles ; the emblems of the Four Evangelists being at the corners.   The book was issued in folio size, and being well printed in fine black Gothic letter presented a handsome appearance.   There seems to be no authority for calling it the "Authorised Version," since, so far as is known, there was no Edict of Convocation, or Act of Parliament, or decision of Privy Council, or royal proclamation giving it authority. The words "Appointed to be read in Churches" mean not *authorised*, but, as explained on a page in the preliminary matter, how the Scriptures were arranged for public reading. In many editions these words were omitted. Possibly it was described as "Authorised" as taking the place, and consequently assuming the privileges, of the Bishops' Bible by which it was preceded.

There seem to have been two impressions of the first edition of 1611, probably due to the impossibility of one printing office being able to supply in the time allotted the 20,000 copies required. The pair are distinct throughout every leaf and are the parents of millions of our Bibles. They are distinguished by calling the first the GREAT HEE BIBLE, and the other the GREAT SHE BIBLE, from their respective readings of Ruth iii. 15, the one reading "he measured six *measures* of barley, and laid *it* on her: and HEE went into the city." The other has "and SHE went into the city." These two editions, both standard but varying in many places, seem to have been deposited in two different printing houses as standard *copy*, for the subsequent editions in quarto and octavo, run in pairs, *he* and *she*, and as a rule the faults of each follow those of its own office-copy. The "She" Bible has a yet more distinctive mark in translating Matthew xxvi. 36, "Then cometh *Judas* [instead of *Jesus*] unto a place called Gethsemane." The "He" Bible is by some regarded as the true first edition, and as giving the true reading, and on this point is sustained by the

Revised Version of 1881. On the other hand the "She" Bible is in accord with almost every other edition. In 1612 the original folio was followed by a quarto edition in Roman type, and also by one in octavo resembling in appearance the octavo copies of the Genevan Version. In that year also appeared the first quarto New Testament; it was not however the first separate New Testament of King James's Version, for a duodecimo edition had been published in 1611.

The two ancient Universities, which in so enterprising a manner produced the most recent Revised Version of 1881, rendered important service also in reprints of the Authorised Version by which it was preceded. In 1629 there appeared the first complete edition of King James's Version ever printed at Cambridge. A separate New Testament in 32mo was, however, printed there the previous year. The 1629 edition had undergone very careful revision, great care also had been exercised in the matter of punctuation and as to the words to be printed in italics. In 1638 appeared the first folio edition of the "Authorised Version" printed at Cambridge. This again gave evidence of careful and extensive revision of the text, italics, and marginal readings, and it remained the standard text until the publication of the Cambridge edition of 1762. In this edition, however, in spite of all the care, appeared the reading in Acts vi. 3 "whom *ye* may appoint," instead of "whom *we*" &c.

THE HOLY
BIBLE
CONTAINING THE
OLD TESTAMENT
AND THE NEW:

*Newly translated out
of the originall tongues:
and with the former
translations diligently
compared and revised
by his Majesties speciall
command.*

Appointed to be read
in Churches.

*Printed by Tho: and John Buck,
printers to the University of
Cambridge.*

As this reading gave power of appointment of officers to the people rather than to the Apostles, the alteration has often been ascribed to the Puritans, and was reputed to have cost Cromwell a bribe of £1000. Yet here it was in 1638 and before Long Parliament days.

The "Standard Edition," as it has been called, of 1762, prepared by Dr Thomas Paris of Trinity College, Cambridge, was issued from the University Press in four volumes, folio. In this, again, a further serious attempt was made to correct the text, by amending the spelling and punctuation, regulating the use of italics and removing printers' errors. Marginal notes, also, were received into the place they have since occupied, and were much extended. The greater part of this impression of 1762 was destroyed by a fire at Dod's the bookseller. To pass by intervening editions a high place for care and laborious exactness must be assigned to the Cambridge Paragraph Bible (in three parts, 1870-3), edited by Dr Scrivener. This has ever since been regarded, as for correctness, the standard text of the Authorised Version. Within the last few years (1903—1905), also, Dr Scrivener has published an edition in five volumes, folio, of King James's Version, "with the Text revised by a Collation of its early and other principal editions." This work deserves special mention for several reasons, and certainly not least for this, that it is a superb piece of typography. It was edited for the Syndics of the University Press, Cambridge, and was printed at the press founded by Mr Cobden Sanderson at Hammersmith. The type was designed by Mr Emery Walker in imitation of the beautiful fount of type used by Jenson, the famous Venetian printer in 1472. The book has been well described as one of the most beautiful Bibles ever printed.

Mention may also be made of the fact that, by way of celebrating the Tercentenary of the Authorised Version, Dr Aldis Wright, Vice-Master of Trinity College, Cambridge, has issued an edition in five volumes, giving an absolutely faithful reproduction of the original text; the text reprinted being that of the *first* of the two issues of 1611.

It was not till 1675 that the sister University of Oxford entered upon the work of Bible publication. In that year appeared in quarto the Holy Bible, printed "At the Theater Oxford." A second edition from the same press came out in 1679, and among the booksellers' names on the title-page is that of Thomas Guy, "at the corner of Little Lumbard Street," who had grown rich by the trade in Bibles, had increased his wealth by successful speculation in South Sea Stock, and, before his death in 1724, founded the great Hospital known by his name.

Three years later the Oxford Press sent forth its first folio reprint of the Authorised Version; this being followed by an Imperial folio copy printed at the same press by John Baskett. The latter was a magnificent edition printed in large type and illustrated by many plates engraved on steel. It came however to be nicknamed the Vinegar Bible, because the headline of Luke xxii. reads "the parable of the *Vinegar*" instead of the *Vineyard.* Of this most sumptuous of all the Oxford Bibles three copies at least were printed on vellum. Unfortunately its fine appearance was discounted by so many misprints that it acquired another nickname and came to be called from its printer "a *Baskett*-full of printers' errors."

In 1769 there came out another folio copy known as the Oxford "Standard Edition," edited and revised by Dr Benjamin Blayney of Hertford College, who followed the lines of Dr Paris' Cambridge edition of 1762. This and the quarto edition, commonly called Dr Blayney's editions, were adopted as standards by the University Press, Oxford, in 1769, and are still the Oxford Standard. In 1833, when Samuel Collingwood and Co. were the University printers, there was sent forth in quarto an edition with the title: "The Holy Bible, an exact reprint, page for page, of the Authorised Version published in the year 1611." And now in this Tercentenary year there has again been issued "a reproduction in Roman type, page for page, of King James's Bible, as published in 1611," with a bibliographical introduction by Mr A. W. Pollard.

Turning back to the past for a moment we find that in 1633 there was printed in Scotland by Robert Young, a Londoner, the first edition of King James's version which then began to supplant the Genevan version in the north.   In 1714 the earliest edition of the same version was printed in Ireland; and in 1782, a duodecimo edition of the earliest English Bible, avowedly printed in America, came from the press of R. Aitken in Philadelphia.   This was followed in 1793 by one printed in Worcester, Massachusetts, by Isaiah Thomas, whom Benjamin Franklin called the "Baskerville of America."

Beyond such details as these just given it is not possible to follow all the fortunes of the Great Version of 1611.   The catalogue of the Library of the British and Foreign Bible Society enumerates nearly a thousand separate editions of the English Bible, or of some part of it published before the close of the 18th century, and this one Society has since its foundation in 1804, sent out in English alone no fewer than seventy-two millions of copies.   The appearance of this version, therefore, is one of the great facts in the history of the world.   What it has been in personal life and character, in the family, in the history of churches and nations can only be known when the great day of final revelation shall come.

CHAPTER VII

THE REVISED VERSION OF 1881

THE Authorised Version of 1611, whose history we have followed, won its way gradually to national acceptance, and did so not because invested with royal authority, but by virtue of its own intrinsic excellence. Its one and only competitor of influential sort was the Genevan version which was still in great favour with many. Indeed, the same year in which the new revision appeared, two other editions of the Genevan, a folio and a quarto, were published by the King's printer ; and for five years more, further editions continued to be sent forth. Then, too, even after 1616, when it ceased to be printed in England, it continued to be printed abroad and sent over to this country. But at length this competition came to an end, the Revision of 1611 obtained wider acceptance and soon became without question the Bible of the English people.

Still, as the book became better known the question of further revision began to be discussed.

8—2

There is no finality in human affairs, and each generation has to take its own part and place in the general advance. Deepening acquaintance led to deeper certainty that, in spite of all the care which had been taken, numerous errors, verbal and otherwise, had been retained in the version so recently revised. And others came to be added from time to time as new editions, edited with insufficient care, were sent forth into the world. For example, the edition of 1631 acquired the name of "the wicked Bible," because it read "thou shalt commit adultery," instead of "thou shalt *not.*" In editions of 1638 it was stated that "the fire devoured 2050 men," instead of 250; "He slew two lions like men," instead of "two lion-like men"; "taught by the people of men," for "by the precept of men." These are only a few examples out of many, and the list was made longer by the importation of Bibles from abroad. The printers of Amsterdam made the discovery that Bible-printing might be developed into a lucrative business, and sent over considerable consignments to this country. It scarcely needs to be pointed out that English Bibles set up by Dutch compositors were not likely to be productions of unfailing accuracy. The process went on so long and so far that in 1643 the Assembly of Divines at Westminster found it necessary to make a report to Parliament on the subject, giving instances of mistakes which had been made, such as "found the rulers" for "found the mules"; "corruption" for "conception"; "condemnation" for "redemption." It was resolved in consequence that foreign Bibles should not be sold until they had been "passed and allowed." It was stated in 1646, at Amsterdam, that an English printer there had sent out in five years 40,000 copies; that his last edition consisted of 12,000 copies, and that altogether in that Dutch city 150,000 English Bibles had been printed.

In Bibles also produced in this country as well as in those sent from abroad new errors were made and old ones copied from one to another. A considerable sheaf of mistakes, such as the following, came to be gathered by observant readers: "shall glean" for "shall *not* glean"; "in the throne of David" for "in the room of David"; "shined through darkness" for "walked through darkness"; "delighted herself" for "defiled herself"; and "I praise you" for "I praise you not." This kind of process went on year after year, repeating itself and extending itself. When Dr Scrivener set about making the Cambridge Paragraph Bible of 1873 as strictly accurate as possible, the changes, most of them trivial, but many not trivial, which had to be made in the text, were to be counted by hundreds.

Then too, as another reason for revision, language itself undergoes change, and words pass out of use or become unintelligible. So again there are many words which, while still in use, are understood in a different sense from that prevailing in 1611. The translators in writing attached one meaning, we in reading quite another. So that words which once served as stepping-stones to the reader become stumbling-blocks in his path. Instances of this may be found in such cases as where carriage means baggage (Acts xxi. 15); careful, anxious (Phil. iv. 6); liberal, noble and churl, crafty (Isa. xxxii. 5); delicately, luxuriously (Luke vii. 25); and publican, a revenue officer. Then again as to the MSS. of the Greek Text from which translations had to be made. It stands to reason that, in the manuscripts from which we translate, the nearer we get to the time when Gospels and Epistles were written, the more likely we are to get the actual words first written. Now it is well known that what are regarded as the most authoritative MSS. of the Greek Text of the New Testament have, with two exceptions, come to light since the time of the translators of 1611. Of the Uncial manuscripts the most ancient and important are: the *Sinaitic*, written in the 4th century, and now deposited in the Imperial Library at St Petersburg; the *Vatican*, also of the 4th century, and preserved in the Vatican Library at Rome; the *Alexandrine* of the 5th century, now in the British Museum; the *Ephraem Codex* of the 5th century, in the National Library at Paris; *Beza's Codex* of the 6th century, in the University Library,

Cambridge; and the *Claromontane*, also of the 6th century, which formerly belonged to Beza, but is now in the National Library at Paris. Yet not one of these was available at the time when King James's translation was made. The Vatican MS., one of the two oldest, though known to be in existence as early as 1587 was so jealously guarded at the Vatican, so far as the New Testament was concerned, that not till the first half of last century could its text be ascertained and then only by a comparison of three more or less imperfect collations. Whereas now we have a magnificent reproduction in photographic facsimile of the entire MS. The Sinaitic MS., also of the 4th century, was discovered by Dr Tischendorf as recently as Feb. 4th, 1859. The Alexandrine was not brought to light until 1628 when it was presented to Charles I by Cyril Lucar, patriarch of Constantinople. And although the Ephraem Codex was brought to Europe in the early part of the 16th century, it was not known to contain a portion of the New Testament until towards the close of the 17th century, and was not collated until 1716. Then, too, MSS. are not our only source of knowledge of the original text of the Scriptures. There are ancient versions such as the Old Latin, the Old Syriac and the two Egyptian versions, all of which came to be accessible to the scholars of the 19th century as they were not to the revisers of 1611, and from their early date must have been made from the earliest manuscripts and were likely therefore to furnish, in the case of disputed passages, valuable suggestions as to the actual words employed at first. Thus the possession of greatly improved apparatus furnished an additional reason for undertaking a further revision.

By the time that the Authorised Version was forty years old men's thoughts began to be turned to the subject. As early as 1655 the Long Parliament made an order that a Bill should be brought in for a new translation of the Bible, and four years later the House directed "that it be referred to a Committee to send for and advise with Dr Walton, Dr Cudworth and others such as they should think fit, and to consider of the translations and impressions of the Bible and to offer their opinions therein." The Committee met from time to time at the house of Bulstrode Whitelocke, but eventually the death of Cromwell put an end to all further endeavours in the way of revision.

Nothing was done, as we might expect, after the coming in of the Restoration, but in the 18th century various tentative efforts were made, some of them by able men. Revised translations of the New Testament were made by Gilbert Wakefield in 1795; by Archbishop Newcome in 1796; and by Scarlett in 1798. But then came the French Revolution and frightened Englishmen. In 1796 the note of alarm was sounded in a letter to the Bishop of Ely, and, as Dr Plumptre has said: "from that time conservatism pure and simple was in the ascendant. To suggest that the Authorised Version might be inaccurate, was almost as bad as holding 'French Principles.'"

When we pass into the 19th century the long-defeated hope was revived by the appearance of Lectures in 1810 by the Lady Margaret Professor of Divinity at Cambridge, Dr Marsh, afterwards Bishop of Peterborough. In his first edition he plainly said: "It is probable that our Authorised Version is as faithful a representation of the original Scriptures as *could* have been formed at *that period*. But when we consider the immense accession that has *since* been made, both to our critical and philological apparatus; when we consider that the most important sources of intelligence for the *interpretation* of the original Scriptures were *likewise* opened after that period, we cannot possibly pretend that our Authorised Version does not require *amendment*"; the italics here given are the Professor's own. Forty-six years later the Rev. Wm. Selwyn, another Lady Margaret Professor of Divinity at Cambridge, spoke out to the same effect. In a work of his entitled "Notes on the proposed Amendment of the Authorised Version of the Holy Scriptures," he said: "I do not hesitate to avow my firm persuasion that there are at least one thousand passages of the English Bible that might be amended without any change in the general texture and justly reverenced language of the version." Professor Selwyn also brought the subject of revision before the Lower House of Convocation of the Province of Canterbury; and that same year, 1856, Mr Heywood, M.P. for North Lancashire, moved in the House of Commons an Address to the Crown praying that Her Majesty would appoint a Royal Commission of learned men to consider of such amendments of the Authorised Version of the Bible as had been already proposed, and to receive suggestions from all persons who might be willing to offer them, and to report the amendments which they might be prepared to recommend.

About the same time also there was published a translation of "The Gospel of John newly compared with the original Greek and revised by five clergymen." The five clergymen were Dr John Barrow, George Moberly, D.C.L., Henry Alford, B.D., W. G. Humphrey, B.D., and Charles J. Ellicott, M.A., their purpose being to show by example the kind of thing in the way of revision many were desiring to see. That same year, also, Dr Trench, then Dean of Westminster, published his work "On the Authorised Version of the New Testament," pleading for movement in the same direction.

The first actual step was taken on February 10,

1870, when a resolution was moved in the Upper House of Convocation by Bishop Wilberforce and seconded by Bishop Ellicott, that a committee of both Houses be appointed to report upon the desirableness of a revision of the Authorised Version of the New Testament. On the motion of Bishop Ollivant seconded by Bishop Thirlwall it was agreed to enlarge this resolution so as to include the Old Testament also, and the resolution so amended was ultimately adopted, and communicated to the Lower House the following day, where it was accepted without a division.

The Committee thus appointed, consisting of seven Bishops and fourteen members of the Lower House, met on March 24 and agreed to report: That it was desirable that a revision be undertaken; that it should comprise both marginal readings and such emendations in the text of the Authorised Version as may be found necessary; that it should not contemplate any new translation of the Bible, or any alteration of the language except where, in the judgment of the most competent scholars, such change is necessary; and that where such change was made the language of the existing version should be closely followed; finally that it was desirable that Convocation should nominate a body of its own Members to undertake the work of revision, who shall be at liberty to invite the co-operation of any eminent for scholarship, to whatever nation or religious body they may belong.

This Report was presented to the Upper House on May 3rd, where its adoption was carried unanimously, and a committee appointed to carry it into effect. In the Lower House an attempt was made to confine the revision to scholars in communion with the Church of England. This however was unsuccessful and the adoption of the Report was carried with two dissentients only. The joint Committee held their first meeting on May 25th and agreed to separate into two Companies—one for the revision of the Old Testament and one for that of the New. They also selected the scholars who should be invited to join the Companies and decided upon the general rules which should guide their procedure.

The rules agreed upon were: To introduce as few alterations as possible consistent with faithfulness; to keep as far as possible to the language of the Authorised and earlier versions; each Company to go twice over the portion to be revised; the Text to be adopted to be that for which the evidence is decidedly preponderating; to make or retain no change in the Text on the second and final revision by each Company, except *two-thirds* of those present approve of the same; to revise the headings of chapters, pages, paragraphs, italics and punctuation; and, finally to refer on the part of each Company, when considered desirable, to divines, scholars and literary men, whether at home or abroad, for their opinions.

The Old Testament Company as at first constituted consisted of twenty-four members; an equal number acted also for the New Testament. In the course of the ten years they were at work changes from various causes had to be made, and ultimately the revisers consisted of sixty-five English scholars who took part in the work. Of these forty-one were members of the Church of England, and twenty-four members of other churches. Of the latter number two represented the Episcopal Church of Ireland, one the Episcopal Church of Scotland, four the Baptists, three the Congregationalists, five the Free Church of Scotland, five the Established Church of Scotland, one the United Presbyterians, one the Unitarians, and two the Wesleyan Methodists.

Varied representation was still further secured by the co-operation of a number of American scholars, selected and invited by the Rev. Dr Schaff of New York, acting on behalf of the English Companies. Various causes of delay, however, intervened, and it was not until July 17, 1872, that the communication was made that the American Companies were duly constituted. It thus came about that the English revisers of the Old Testament had already made some progress, had in fact gone twice through the

Pentateuch before they secured the co-operation of the American Old Testament Revision Company.

The English New Testament Company assembled for the first time on Wednesday, June 22, 1870. They met in the Chapel of Henry VII, and there united in the celebration of the Lord's Supper. After this act of worship they formally entered upon the task assigned them.

Through the kind arrangement of Dr Stanley, then Dean of Westminster, the Jerusalem Chamber of the Abbey was assigned as their place of meeting. This room, as Dr Newth one of the revisers reminded us, is one of more than ordinary interest. Originally the parlour of the Abbot's palace, it was here the Assembly of Divines of Commonwealth days, driven by the cold from Henry VII's Chapel, held its 66th session, on October 2nd, 1643, and there thenceforward continned to meet until its closing session on February 22nd, 1649. Here were prepared the Westminster Confession of Faith and the Longer and Shorter Catechisms which formerly played so conspicuous a part in the religious education of the Presbyterians of Scotland and the Independents of England. And here, also, just fifty years later, assembled the Commission appointed by William III to devise a basis for a scheme of comprehension in a revision of the Prayer Book. It was in this same room the New Testament Company held their meetings for ten years, except on the few occasions when it was not available.

Dr Newth has further told us of the method of procedure. The Company assembled at eleven a.m. and continued in session till six p.m., with an interval of half an hour. Prayer being offered, and preliminary matters of correspondence disposed of, the Chairman read a short passage as given in the Authorised Version. The question was then asked, first, as to *textual* changes ; that being settled the Chairman asked for proposals of rendering, and free discussion having followed, the vote of the Company was taken. They resolved the work should be thoroughly done, but eventually grew alarmed at the probable length of time the revision would take.

At the end of the ninth day of meeting, not more than 153 verses had been revised, an average of only seventeen verses a day. By and by, however, progress became more rapid, but even then the average did not rise above thirty-five verses a day. The first revision of the Gospel of Matthew was completed on the 36th day of meeting, May 24th, 1871, and that of John on the 103rd day, February 19th, 1873. The first revision of the Apocalypse, the final book, was completed on the 273rd meeting, April 20th, 1877. The meetings were held monthly for a session of four consecutive days, excepting only August and September. Thus the first revision required 241

meetings, during sixty monthly sessions ; the second
revision was completed on December 13th, 1878,
having occupied on the whole 96 meetings or about
two years and a half. Then came the suggestions of
the American Company for consideration, and these,
together with the preparation of the preface, occupied
the Company until November 11th, 1880, on which
day, at five o'clock in the afternoon, after ten years
and five months of labour, the revision of the New
Testament was brought to its close. On the evening
of that same day, being St Martin's day, the Company assembled in the church of St Martin's-in-the-
Fields and there united in a special service of prayer
and thanksgiving—*Thanksgiving* for the happy completion of their labours, for the spirit of harmony and
brotherly affection that had pervaded their meetings,
and for the Divine goodness which had permitted so
many to give themselves continuously to this work,
and *Prayer* that He whose glory they had humbly
striven to promote might graciously accept this their
service, and deign to use it as an instrument for the
good of man and the honour of His holy name. The
New Testament was published on May 17th, 1881,
and that same day was also presented to the Queen.

The Revision of the Old Testament, being of a
much larger book, took longer time than that of the
New; but in one important respect the work was
much simpler than that which the New Testament

Company had before them. They had no difficulty in determining the Original Text from which to translate, whereas in the case of the New Testament that was often matter for anxious and prolonged consideration. The Received, or, as it is commonly called, the Massoretic Text of the Old Testament Scriptures, has come down to us in manuscripts which are of no great antiquity. The earliest of which the age is known is as late as A.D. 916, and they all belong to the same family or recension. That there were other recensions at one time is probable from the fact that there are variations in the ancient Versions, the oldest of which, the Greek Septuagint, was, in part at least, made over two centuries before the Christian era. But as the state of our knowledge on this subject is not at present such as to justify any attempt at an entire reconstruction of the text on the authority of these Versions, the revisers felt it most prudent, as they tell us, simply to adopt the Massoretic Text as the basis of their work, and, following the example of the translators of the Authorised Version, to depart from it only in exceptional cases. The Revision of the Old Testament was commenced on the 30th of June, 1870, and was completed in eighty-five sessions, occupying 792 days, and ending on 20th June, 1884. The greater part of the sessions were for ten days each, and each day the Company generally sat for six hours. The labour therefore was great, but ungrudg-

B.

ingly rendered, and the revisers, like their brethren of the New Testament Company, brought their long task to a close with a feeling of deep thankfulness to Almighty God, and the earnest hope that their endeavours might with His blessing tend to a clearer knowledge of the Old Testament Scriptures.

The revision of the Authorised Version of the Apocrypha was included in the arrangement between the Companies and the Representatives of the Presses of Oxford and Cambridge, the publishers and proprietors of the New Version. But this last portion of the work was not to be undertaken until the other and greater portions of the work were concluded. As early, however, as March 21, 1879, it was resolved that after such conclusion, the Company should be divided into three Committees, to be called the London, Westminster and Cambridge Committees, whose work should be the revision of the Apocrypha also. This was done, and thus in 1895 was completed the work begun in hope and prayer no less than five and twenty years before. This work in its completed form as a revision of the great version of 1611 has been spreading more and more widely among the Christian people of the land. It has not escaped criticism, no work of man's hand can hope to do that. In many ways it is open to criticism, but it has made a new Bible for many, and made plainer to them the revelation of the mind of God. What does this renders effectual service to humanity. The Bible is the greatest of all great books. "There are many echoes in the world," said Goethe, "but few voices." This book is a living voice carrying its own authority with it. As the Confession of Faith of the Scottish Church declared: "Amongst the arguments whereby the Holy Scripture doth abundantly evidence itself to be the Word of God are the heavenliness of the matter, the efficacy of the doctrine, the majesty of the style, the consent of all the parts, the scope of the whole."

BIBLIOGRAPHY

Historical Catalogue of the printed Editions of Holy Scripture in the Library of the British and Foreign Bible Society. Compiled by T. H. Darlow and H. F. Moule. Vol. I. English, 1903, 4to.

Catalogue of an Exhibition of Bibles in the John Rylands Library, Manchester, illustrating the history of the English versions from Wiclif to the present time, 1904.

Catalogue of the Caxton Celebration of 1877: Class C, Holy Scriptures and Liturgies.

Description of the Great Bible, 1539, and the six Editions of Cranmer's Bible, 1540 and 1541, printed by Grafton and Whitchurch; also of the Editions in large folio of the Authorised Version of the Holy Scriptures, printed in the years 1611, 1613, 1617, 1634, 1640. London, 1865, fol. By Francis Fry.

Hastings' Dictionary of the Bible—Extra Volume. Versions (English), by J. H. Lupton.

Encyclopaedia Britannica, 11th Edition—The English Bible, by Anna C. Paues, Ph.D., and H. H. Henson, D.D.

A General View of the history of the English Bible. Third Edition, revised by W. Aldis Wright, 1905.

Lectures on Bible Revision, by Samuel Newth, D.D., 1881.

Our English Bible: its Translations and Translators, by John Stoughton, D.D., 1878.

The History of the English Bible, by W. F. Moulton, D.D. New Edition.

A Fourteenth Century English Biblical Version. Edited by Anna C. Paues. Cambridge, 1904.

The Holy Gospels in Anglo-Saxon. Edited by W. W. Skeat, 1871—1877.

The Holy Bible...in the earliest English versions made from the Latin Vulgate by John Wycliffe and his followers. Edited by...Josiah Forshall...and Sir Frederick Madden. Oxford, 1850. 4 Vols. 4to.

The Cambridge Paragraph Bible, with Revised Text and Critical Introduction by F. H. Scrivener. Cambridge, 1873.

The part of Rheims in the making of the English Bible, by J. G. Carleton. Oxford, 1902.

A Century of Bibles of the Authorised Version from 1611 to 1711, by W. J. Loftie, 1872.

The English Bible, 2 vols., 1876, by J. Eadie.

History of the English Bible, by T. H. Pattison, 1894.

The first printed English New Testament. E. Arber, 1871.

Our Bible and the Ancient Manuscripts, by F. G. Kenyon, 1895.

INDEX

CAMBRIDGE: PRINTED BY JOHN CLAY, M.A. AT THE UNIVERSITY PRESS

THE
CAMBRIDGE MANUALS
OF SCIENCE AND LITERATURE

Published by the Cambridge University Press

GENERAL EDITORS

P. GILES, Litt.D.
Master of Emmanuel College

and

A. C. SEWARD, M.A., F.R.S.
Professor of Botany in the University of Cambridge

VOLUMES NOW READY

The Coming of Evolution. By Prof. J. W. Judd, C.B., F.R.S.

Heredity in the Light of Recent Research. By L. Doncaster, M.A.

The English Puritans. By the Rev. John Brown, D.D.

The Idea of God in Early Religions. By Dr F. B. Jevons.

Plant-Animals: a Study in Symbiosis. By Prof. F. W. Keeble, Sc.D.

Cash and Credit. By D. A. Barker, I.C.S.

The Natural History of Coal. By Dr E. A. Newell Arber.

The Early Religious Poetry of the Hebrews. By the Rev. E. G. King, D.D.

The History of the English Bible. By the Rev. John Brown, D.D.

Plant-Life on Land. By Prof. F. O. Bower, Sc.D., F.R.S.

An Historical Account of the Rise and Development of Presbyterianism in Scotland. By the Rt Hon. the Lord Balfour of Burleigh, K.T., G.C.M.G.

English Dialects from the Eighth Century to the Present Day. By the Rev. Prof. W. W. Skeat, Litt.D., D.C.L., F.B.A.

The Administration of Justice in Criminal Matters (in England and Wales). By G. Glover Alexander, M.A., LL.M.

VOLUMES NOW READY (*continued*)

An Introduction to Experimental Psychology. By Dr C. S. Myers.

The Ground Plan of the English Parish Church. By A. Hamilton Thompson, M.A., F.S.A.

The Historical Growth of the English Parish Church. By A. Hamilton Thompson, M.A., F.S.A.

Aerial Locomotion. By E. H. Harper, M.A., and Allan E. Ferguson, B.Sc.

Electricity in Locomotion. By A. G. Whyte, B.Sc.

New Zealand. By the Hon. Sir Robert Stout, K.C.M.G., LL.D., and J. Logan Stout, LL.B. (N.Z.).

King Arthur in History and Legend. By Prof. W. Lewis Jones, M.A.

The Early Religious Poetry of Persia. By the Rev. Prof. J. Hope Moulton, D.D., D.Theol. (Berlin).

Greek Tragedy. By J. T. Sheppard, M.A.

The Wanderings of Peoples. By Dr A. C. Haddon, F.R.S.

Links with the Past in the Plant-World. By Prof. A. C. Seward, F.R.S.

Primitive Animals. By Geoffrey Smith, M.A.

Life in the Sea. By James Johnstone, B.Sc.

The Moral Life and Moral Worth. By Prof. Sorley, Litt.D., F.B.A.

The Migration of Birds. By T. A. Coward.

Earthworms and their Allies. By F. E. Beddard, M.A., F.R.S.

Prehistoric Man. By Dr W. L. H. Duckworth.

The Modern Locomotive. By C. Edgar Allen, A.M.I.Mech.E.

The Natural History of Clay. By Alfred B. Searle.

The Origin of Earthquakes. By Dr C. Davison.

The Ballad in Literature. By T. F. Henderson.

Ancient Assyria. By Rev. C. H. W. Johns, Litt.D.

The Work of Rain and Rivers. By the Rev. Prof. T. G. Bonney, LL.D., Sc.D., F.R.S.

Rocks and their Origins. By Prof. Grenville A. J. Cole.

A History of Civilization in Palestine. By Prof. R. A. S. Macalister, M.A., F.S.A.

Goethe and the Twentieth Century. By Prof. J. G. Robertson, M.A., Ph.D.

Spiders. By C. Warburton, M.A.

Methodism. By Rev. H. B. Workman, D.Lit.

Life in the Medieval University. By R. S. Rait, M.A.

The Troubadours. By the Rev. H. J. Chaytor, M.A.

Individuality in the Animal Kingdom. By Julian Huxley, B.A.

VOLUMES IN PREPARATION

VOLUMES IN PREPARATION (continued)

Insects as Carriers of Disease. By Prof. G. H. F. Nuttall, F.R.S.
Natural Caves and Fissures. By Dr A. Rule.
Submerged Forests. By Clement Reid, F.R.S.
A Grammar of Heraldry. By W. H. St John Hope, M.A.
Prehistoric Britain. By L. McL. Mann.
The Story of a Loaf of Bread. By Prof. T. B. Wood.
Soil Fertility. By Dr E. J. Russell.
Comparative Religion. By. Prof. F. B. Jevons, Litt.D.

PRESS NOTICES

"For those who have neither the time nor the preliminary training to study great subjects on a grand scale these excellent handbooks seem specially designed. They have been written by scholars of eminence, and give in small compass an admirable epitome of the subjects with which they deal.......These little volumes represent the essence that the specialism of to-day can give to the people in popular form on the subjects dealt with."

Scotsman

"The Cambridge Manuals of Science and Literature have already conquered a wide audience amongst cultured people. They are short studies of great subjects, and are published by the University Press at one shilling ......The Cambridge Press is casting its literary net widely."—*Standard*

"No such masterpieces of concentrated excellence as these Cambridge Manuals have been published since the Literature and Science Primers of about thirty years ago, in which the leading men of that day made complete expositions in miniature of their respective subjects...... The increase of specialisation which is steadily going on enormously enhances the value of manuals such as these, in which an expert who has every detail of a particular subject at his finger ends makes a pithy and luminous summary of it for the enlightenment of the general reader, and enables him to grasp easily the fruit of the work of many minds."

Nottingham Guardian

Cambridge University Press
London : Fetter Lane, E.C.
C. F. Clay, Manager
Edinburgh : 100, Princes Street

ND - #0015 - 230922 - C0 - 229/152/9 [11] - CB - 9780265192634 - Gloss Lamination